DEMOCRACY RISING

POLITICS AND PARTICIPATION IN CANADA

BILL FREEMAN

FOREWORD BY ADAM VAUGHAN

DUNDURN
TORONTO

Printer: Webcom
Cover image: istock.com/ smartboy10

Library and Archives Canada Cataloguing in Publication

Freeman, Bill, 1938-, author
    Democracy rising : politics and participation in Canada / Bill Freeman ; foreword by Adam Vaughan

Includes bibliographical references and index.
Issued in print and electronic formats.

ISBN 978-1-4597-3767-9 (paperback).--ISBN 978-1-4597-3768-6 (PDF).--ISBN 978-1-4597-3769-3 (EPUB)

1. Political participation--Canada. 2. Democracy--Canada. I. Title.

JL186.5.F74 2017   323'.0420971   C2016-907276-2
                                      C2016-907277-0

2   3   4   5   21   20   19   18   17

 Conseil des Arts du Canada   Canada Council for the Arts      ONTARIO ARTS COUNCIL CONSEIL DES ARTS DE L'ONTARIO an Ontario government agency un organisme du gouvernement de l'Ontario

We acknowledge the support of the **Canada Council for the Arts** and the **Ontario Arts Council** for our publishing program. We also acknowledge the financial support of the **Government of Ontario**, through the **Ontario Book Publishing Tax Credit** and the **Ontario Media Development Corporation**, and the **Government of Canada**.

Care has been taken to trace the ownership of copyright material used in this book. The author and the publisher welcome any information enabling them to rectify any references or credits in subsequent editions.
— *J. Kirk Howard, President*

The publisher is not responsible for websites or their content unless they are owned by the publisher.

Printed and bound in Canada.

VISIT US AT

dundurn.com | @dundurnpress | dundurnpress | dundurnpress

Dundurn
3 Church Street, Suite 500
Toronto, Ontario, Canada
M5E 1M2

CONTENTS

FOREWORD

No Is a Very Powerful Word in Politics

We find ourselves in a position where the politics of NO has become the most powerful democratic force. It defies ideology, is both harnessed and unleashed by technology, and has surrendered politics and democracy to a constant state of referendum. It produces simple responses to complex questions and replaces facts with opinions. Slogans matter more than principles.

The science of politics missed this transformation. The art of politics has all but disappeared. The business of politics has taken over now, from consumer tracking and data mining to perpetual fundraising and never-ending campaigns. Politics is only about winning and losing.

Governing has effectively become a business too. Decisions are measured as deals and transaction, politicians branded and prepped for market, citizens asked for input at election time and then left alone until next shopping season. This process is almost designed to breed cynicism. As people disengage other forces take over, and government becomes even easier to ignore. It's as if society is on autopilot.

It isn't.

Never before has the fragility of modern democracy been laid so bare. The problem seems most acute in the English-speaking world, but we are fooling ourselves if recent events in France, Austria, and the Netherlands are not equally disturbing. The rise of populist demagogues, nationalist movements that seek to close borders and close minds to new ideas, are a direct result of the breakdown in the relationship between the governed and the government. Democracy is brittle and we seem determined to let it break, if not break it ourselves.

The danger of trying to rule ourselves this way is that all we do as a body politic, and all we seem to be good at these days, is breaking things;

slashing taxes, cutting programs, ripping up treaties, stopping projects, and, of course, waging an endless war on spending. It's as if reform is impossible, compromise not a noble pursuit, and innovation beyond our capacity. It's a policy that rewards reactionaries and punishes people with ideas. Complexity is rarely tolerated.

In this book, Bill Freeman takes a look at how we got here. He proposes possible ways forward. He explores the roots of how we built our unique form of responsible government in Canada. He argues that we did it through democratic struggle. The process sometimes involved pamphlets and protest. It took rebellion. In the end, focused and principled determination delivered real change. Freeman also notes this remarkable evolution was achieved despite the presence of powerful vested interests at every point in history; he illustrates and champions the idea that it is possible to achieve social justice democratically, through organization from the ground up. He leaves us with the hope that it always was this way and always will be, but it takes more effort than just tweeting about a better tomorrow. It takes actual work.

The book is clear that democratically empowered communities have always had to fight against the entrenched power of a few. That the struggle may not always be obvious but it is a consistent dynamic. Recently this privileged minority has challenged collective action by fuelling a surge of individuality proclaimed as the fight for freedom. It has created new forms of leadership driven by the cult of personality. Freeman looks at how influential elites have acted in concert to reverse decades, if not a century, of reform. These cliques of entrenched interests have a lot to gain if democracy is broken. When not wielding the hammer themselves they are the willing distributors of the tools that allow society to undermine its own institution. The failure of government becomes evidence that government doesn't work, and then more damage can be done as fewer and fewer care.

Freeman is not naive. Nor does he pretend that opposition is not needed. The author is a veteran of organizing people and communities against some very bad ideas and terrible projects created and promoted by democratically elected governments. What Freeman presents is an idea critical for those who are fighting for democracy. The author links the building of political arguments to the act of building democratic society. The act of organizing people to wage campaigns for change is exactly how societies are formed. It's how healthy and progressive democratic governments are both created and sustained.

The act of saying *yes* is not just an option, it's the responsibility that comes with the right to say *no*. You can't destroy what's wrong if you're not committed to creating something better. This is the essence of healthy democratic government.

Ideas are always more powerful than any ideology. Our fragile democracy can be made strong again.

Adam Vaughan
Member of Parliament, Spadina-Fort York

INTRODUCTION

In 2016 two political events have been like an earthquake, shaking the waters of public life. The first was the Brexit vote by the British people to leave the European Union, and the second was the long campaign of Donald Trump and his election to become the president of the United States.

Many political leaders, the corporate elite, and the media have been in a panic. All of their predictions have been wrong. Trump was dismissed at the beginning of the primaries as being a lightweight, and yet he went on to win the presidency of the most influential and powerful country in the world. Britain's exit from the E.U. was thought to be so remote a possibility that a referendum was called to put the issue to rest. It was believed that ordinary people would not leap into the unknown and vote for political options that could lead to chaos and disaster, but in both instances the public defied the elites.

The media is still puzzling over what happened. They blame those who have been economically left behind and say that these votes point to the rising influence of right-wing politics. Age, ignorance, and gender are other factors, apparently. In both Britain and the United States, it was older males lacking post-secondary education who voted for these marginal candidates and causes. In fact, the roots are much broader and deeper than this.

There is a common element that runs through both of these events. Vast numbers of people are fed up with the elites who control the political process and engineer government policy for their own interests. Decisions are being made that threaten their jobs, their families, and their communities, and no one is listening to their concerns. They want it known that they are hurting, and that the political system is not working for them. People are struggling, and their children face a diminished future. They don't like it one bit.

But above all, they are tired of prosperous members of the elite telling them what is good for them and how they should be voting. They have rebelled in the only way they can — the only way the system allows them to rebel — by voting for a know-nothing, self-centred political demagogue, and by rejecting the E.U., a political power centred in Brussels that they know little about.

There is deep dissatisfaction among the followers of the left, right, and centre, and it goes through all parts of the developed world, Canada included. People are not happy with the cozy relationships their governments have with the elites. The message that they have delivered is that they want something done about the way governments are run, or there is going to be hell to pay.

That is what this book is all about. It spends time diagnosing the reasons for the political and social malaise that we are facing, it takes a close look at the groups that have struggled for social change, and it examines the rising demand for a new type of participatory democracy.

The route through this maze is via historical Canadian events and movements, but what is offered is a very different type of history than what you might read in conventional texts. Historical examples are used to demonstrate both how elites built special privileges, and how people have built opposition groups to express their grievances and to right wrongs.

And let me warn you of another somewhat unusual thing that you will come across in this book. The typical view of politics held by Canadians is that it is something restricted to elections, or to the activities in Ottawa, the provincial capitals, or city hall. This is too narrow a view, in my opinion. I believe that politics is an ongoing process that all of us are involved in — whether we know it or not. It happens whenever people talk about political, social, and economic issues that affect us: things like debates at union meetings, discussion of a new development in a neighbourhood, a corporate committee meeting to discuss regulations influencing the company, or a government finance meeting.

The participation of citizens in politics is, or should be, at the core of civic life. The problem is, there are large numbers of people — the vast majority in fact — who have no real ability to influence our political life. Not only are they excluded, but their concerns and issues are ignored. That is the malaise that has affected us. Democracy is the promise of government by the people, but we have developed a government dominated by elites, particularly economic elites. I believe the only way we can change that is by creating a participatory democracy. It is within our grasp, and we must do it.

At heart I am an optimist and this is an optimistic book. There are disturbing things included in these pages that some people will not like. But there is hope, too. And, I must admit, there is also a good deal of personal opinion. Any book like this is hard fact and opinion. Even what a writer chooses to write about and what to ignore is a choice shaped by opinion. But the core idea in this book is "Democracy Rising." The long arc of Canadian history shows that we are developing a more participatory, more inclusive political culture, and this is all to the good. We must do more to make this a truly participatory democracy.

* * *

A POINT OF VIEW

Now that I have thrust myself into this discussion, let me tell you a little about myself so you can see what has shaped my understanding of this country. I have been a writer most of my adult life, but I come out of an academic tradition, like many other writers in this country. I was trained as a sociologist and studied at McMaster in Hamilton. Today I live on Toronto Island — one of the islands just offshore the Toronto mainland and a unique place to view the political scene — but I grew up in London, Ontario. I lived for a time in both Alberta and Nova Scotia, and spent ten years teaching in Montreal. It is hard to get a grasp on this enormous, sprawling country of ours. I don't pretend to understand everything about Canada, but I do have a feel for the country and all of my writing has been about some aspect of Canadian life.

I have written fiction, novels for young people, and books, like this, about politics, but my interest in all of these things is what I describe as a "view from below." It focuses on ordinary people by looking at how history and social experience shape people's lives.

Over my career I have been involved in many different groups. I was an organizer with a welfare rights organization in Hamilton in the early 1970s and active in the NDP in that city. In Montreal I taught at Vanier CÉGEP and was on the local union executive at the college. I participated in the Montreal Citizens' Movement and organized political campaigns. Back in Toronto, I worked for the Bob Rae NDP provincial government for four years, 1991–95, and was assigned as political staff to the minister of municipal affairs, where I learned a lot about community groups and their impact on provincial politics. For decades I have been an active member of the Writers' Union of Canada, and served as its chair in 2004–05.

One of my major preoccupations as a writer has been cities and grassroots organizations. I wrote my dissertation on Local 1005 of the Steelworkers; it was turned into a book titled *1005: Political Life in a Local Union*. My most recent book, *The New Urban Agenda: The Greater Toronto and Hamilton Area*, has material about urban issues and communities.

In recent years, community groups have become a major interest of mine. I have been active in my own community and involved in the long and difficult fight against the Billy Bishop Toronto City Airport. I follow as best I can what is happening in community groups, environmental organizations, and co-ops because I find that world of citizen politics fascinating.

Through my involvement I learned that the practice of politics and community engagement takes an inordinate amount of time and patience. This has led to stress and worry in my life, with more defeats than victories, but along with many others, I have helped to shape decisions that affected communities that were very important to me. In the process, I have made deep and lasting friendships that are central to my life.

I have been a political activist all of my adult life, working in the trenches for political change and that, more than anything else, has shaped my views on democracy, participation, and the ideas in this book.

PART 1

THE RISE OF
REPRESENTATIVE DEMOCRACY

In *The Communist Manifesto*, Karl Marx and Friedrich Engels described the role of government in this way: "The executive of the modern state is nothing but the committee for the management of the common affairs of the ruling class."

Friedrich Hayek, the godfather of right-wing economic neo-liberalism, believed that capitalism could only flourish in democratic societies. Francis Fukuyama, in *The End of History and the Last Man*, pushes this idea even further by claiming that we are witnessing the end of history; liberal democracy linked to capitalism will prevail in the future.

Both the radical left and radical right seem to agree on one thing: capitalism flourishes in modern democracy.

That certainly can be said to be the case in Canada. Representative democracy emerged as a result of many different historical influences, but once it was established, leaders of big business learned very quickly how they could use it to apply pressure and influence to establish their companies, meet their needs, and increase their wealth; that relationship between big business and government continues to this very day.

Active political participation was and is the essential modus operandi of business, as we will see, and it has paid off handsomely for them.

CHAPTER 1

REPRESENTATIVE DEMOCRACY

The democratic countries that have emerged in the developed world have adopted a system of government called *representative democracy*. Citizens elect representatives, like municipal councillors or members of Parliament, to represent their interests in the governing body. This, it is argued, is government by the people, because the election of politicians by their citizens gives them the mandate to govern by passing laws and regulations that must be followed by everyone.

Direct democracy is another form of democracy. In this type of government all members of the group have the right to make decisions on issues. Most community groups and local unions operate in this way. Typically, a notice of a meeting goes out to all members, and those present at the meeting have the right to speak and vote on all motions. A majority of votes binds the organization to the motions.

Virtually all governments use a form of representative democracy, not direct democracy, because it is the only practical way that large groups, like the residents of cities or the citizens of a nation state, can be democratically governed. Switzerland frequently uses referendums, and a number of municipalities in North America sometimes use them to make decisions on controversial issues, and that is a form of direct democracy. Some municipalities in New England in the United States are governed using a form of direct democracy; decisions are made in community meetings where all citizens are eligible to attend and vote. But it would be impractical to run a country the size of Canada in that way.

The argument that I am going to make for participatory democracy in this book is not a proposal to do away with our form of representative democracy. That would lead to chaos. Participatory democracy is an expansion of representative democracy so that it is more accurately reflects the views of the people.

Before discussing how we can do that, let's look at the history of representative democracy and how this form of government came to be adopted in Canada.

* * *

THE ENLIGHTENMENT

The strongest influence that shaped the politics of Western countries came out of the Enlightenment period of the seventeenth and eighteenth centuries. This was a philosophic movement that promoted rational thinking and science, criticized established religions, and attacked the absolute authority of monarchs and any other forms of authoritarian government that were practised in Europe at that time.

John Locke, the most influential of the Enlightenment thinkers in the English-speaking world, based his political ideas on the social contract theory that deals with the question of the legitimacy of the state. It holds that individuals in society have consented to the legitimacy of the state and surrendered some of their rights in return for protection of themselves and the protection of their rights. One set of what were deemed "inalienable" rights was "life, liberty, and property." This theme of the protection of property is a recurring theme among Enlightenment thinkers, and, of course, of capitalism.

Locke was a liberal of his day, although some of his ideas seem intolerant to us — for example, he did not speak out against denying rights to Catholics — but by comparison to his contemporaries he was very liberal. There were other Enlightenment writers who were more revolutionary, like Jean Jacques Rousseau and Thomas Paine. But although Locke was no revolutionary, his ideas had a profound effect on the American Revolution.

What attracts me to the philosophers of the Enlightenment is that they had an optimistic view of individuals and society. Also, they were egalitarian.

John Locke and others believed that at birth the mind was a tabula rasa (blank slate). He held that everyone starts out the same, and it is society that accords wealth, prestige, and influence to some but leaves others in poverty. That was a very radical idea at the time, when the theory of the divine right of kings and domination of the aristocracy was the official ideology. The belief in equality is a fundamental democratic principle.

* * *

PARLIAMENT, CONFEDERACY, AND THE SOVEREIGN COUNCIL

The other major influence in the development of our representative democracy in the English-speaking world was the growth of Parliament. This began in the thirteenth century as various powerful barons struggled for power against an unpopular king. The barons ultimately forced the king to sign Magna Carta (the Great Charter), which protected the rights of aristocrats. Gradually, rights were strengthened and councils of lords and commoners evolved into the Parliament we know today.

The teaching of British history usually focuses on the growth of Parliament, the struggle between Parliament and the king, and the gradual emergence of parliamentary, or representative democracy, where the rights of individuals are protected by law. It is a fascinating story. Similar struggles were going on in other European countries and other types of societies.

The Iroquois Confederacy, for example, had a form of government not unlike representative democracy, which goes back, some believe, to the twelfth century, long before Europeans ever came to this part of North America. The confederacy was made up of five (later six) nations with a similar culture who spoke different dialects of the Iroquoian language. It was governed by a council of chiefs, each representing a clan. Women had great prestige in Iroquoian culture and often made many of the political decisions.

The Iroquoian Confederacy was a type of federated political system with independent nations that had their own political decision-making bodies. It had influence in the formation of the United States, which is a federation of different states. Canada was influenced by the Iroquois Confederacy indirectly, too, because it is a federated nation with its provinces and territories.

England had a Parliament with a separate House of Commons and House of Lords before English settlers came to North America, but it was hardly a democracy. English political practices came across the Atlantic with the settlers and helped to shape the politics of the Thirteen Colonies. Governors were appointed by the Crown, who then set up the legislatures in the colonies. Although these representatives were elected by the people, in every case the franchise was restricted to male property owners.

New France, founded even before the English settlers came to North America, was also shaped by the political practices of its home country. France in the seventeenth century was dominated by kings who ruled as absolute monarchs. Such was the power and prestige of Louis XIV, for instance, that he called himself the Sun King.

A type of royal government was established in New France after 1663. The governor was responsible directly to the king. He governed through the Sovereign Council made up of himself, the Intendant (responsible for the daily affairs of the colony), seigneurs (landowners), and the Bishop of Quebec. At most about a dozen officials governed the colony. The governor was responsible for defence, a constant worry in a colony with a small population strung out along the St. Lawrence River that was open to attack by the Iroquois and raids from the English. However, the real power lay with the Intendant, who made decisions on everything from commerce to land rights in the colony.

New France was hardly democratic, but then France and the other European countries, including England, were not democratic at that time either. There was, however, considerable local autonomy in the French colony. The habitants had to look after themselves, helped by a few soldiers sent over by the king. That the colony survived at all is testament to the tenacity of the people.

European countries had a variety of political systems of absolute monarchy until late in the eighteenth century, and much later in eastern and southern Europe, but the reality is that even the most autocratic monarchs could never govern alone. They needed councils or parliaments of various sorts just to provide information about what was going on in the country, and they needed advisors who could create and administer appropriate laws.

The first real democratic experiment in North America was played out during the American Revolution, and it is worth looking at this event because it was during this time that the struggle between elites and the people unfolded in public view.

* * *

DEBATING THE AMERICAN CONSTITUTION

The American Revolution and the effort to draft the Constitution are interpreted by popular historians as struggles for democracy. That is true, but it was much more complicated than this. There is even some debate as to which group actually prevailed in the effort to draft the Constitution, the democrats or the elite.

The Revolution was an uprising against an unpopular king, George III, and against laws imposed arbitrarily by the British government on the colonists. "No taxation without representation" was the popular slogan, and that is a demand for democratic rights. The revolution started as a movement to reform the way the colonies were governed and administered, but when the British overreacted by sending troops it became an armed rebellion — one that finally resulted in the victory of the American citizen army with the help of French regular troops at Yorktown, in Virginia.

The army of General George Washington was made up largely of farmers and artisans — the ordinary people who are the foot soldiers of all armies — but once the war was concluded, debate turned to the question of what type of government was appropriate for the American people living in the Thirteen Colonies strung along the Atlantic seaboard. It was the middle- and upper-class lawyers, politicians, merchants, and businessmen who took over this debate while the farmers and workers went back to the task of earning a living. Other large groups of Americans were also ignored: women, slaves, and aboriginal peoples. This was a debate among the elite.

The discussion on the Constitution was spirited and open, conducted in various assemblies and publications. Many opinions were expressed. The core of the debate was around the appropriate structure of government, particularly state rights versus the rights, or powers, of the federal government. That has remained an issue in American politics from that time to today. But there was another issue that is best described as a struggle between those who supported democracy and those who favoured government by an elite, between those who wanted political power to be dispersed widely and those who were concerned about the protection of property.

The group who saw the chief issue as the protection of property and wealth were concerned about the "unchecked rule of the masses," as John Jay, a journalist, diplomat, and judge, wrote. "The people who own the country ought to govern it." Jay and his like-minded allies were concerned that the majority would use their power at the ballot box to take the wealth of the affluent. To them, liberty was linked to property, not democracy, and they sought means to set up structures within government to protect their property.

Jeremy Belknap, at the time a prominent clergyman and historian, wrote that "government originates from the people, but let the people be taught ... that they are unable to govern themselves." He argued that the people should retreat to the margins, understanding their incapacity to govern themselves.

In *The Federalist Papers*, Alexander Hamilton, James Madison, and Jay argued that the new country needed a strong national government that would prevent factions from taking control. They supported representative government, instead of pure democracy, as the structure best able to ensure stability and "prevent temporary passions from setting the course for the nation." In entry number 35 Alexander Hamilton argued that the common people were incapable of serving in Congress. "Their habits in life have not been such as to give them those acquired endowments ... in a deliberative assembly." In other words, no matter how smart a common man was, he did not have enough polish — he lacked the proper grooming — to participate in politics.

The elitism expressed by the so-called Federalists was opposed by those who supported a more truly democratic form of government. Richard Henry Lee, a prominent politician from Virginia who participated actively in all the debates, believed representative government was a "transfer of power from the many to the few." He was concerned that "the Federalists sought to insert an aristocratic political order." Thomas Jefferson also sided with the democrats. He said, "I know no safe depositary of the ultimate powers of society but the people themselves." But he believed they needed improvement. "Self-government is not possible unless the citizens are educated sufficiently to enable them to exercise oversight."[1]

It would be wrong to say that one side prevailed over the other in this debate. What emerged was a type of compromise. But you can see the influence of those who wanted to protect property and wealth in the complicated structure of American government. The House of Representatives is elected directly by the people every two years. There are only two senators for every state and the length of their term is six years, and the practice early in the republic was for states to appoint their senators. They were not elected by the people. Also, presidents are not elected directly by the people; all presidential elections are decided in what is known as the Electoral College. At the time of the drafting of the Constitution, only the House of Representatives was directly elected by the people.

This complicated structure was designed to make government cumbersome and thwart democratic control by the people. Today the power in Congress has shifted away from the House of Representatives. (Some would deny the House has ever been representative because of the gerrymandering of districts.) Senators today are elected by popular vote, but the practice of having only two senators for every state means that small states can outvote states with large populations. And the Electoral College system is still not representative of the people. In the 2016 presidential election Hilary Clinton received two million more votes than Donald Trump, but Trump became the president because he won more Electoral College votes.

The United States was one of the first democracies, and it has developed into a very remarkable country, but its Constitution has led to a political system dominated by corporations and the wealthy. Political alienation is widespread in the United States. It will be very difficult to change the way Americans practise politics because of the rigidity of their Constitution.

* * *

REVOLUTION AND REPRESSION

The French Revolution, that cataclysmic event of the late eighteenth century, erupted less than ten years after the Battle of Yorktown, which concluded the American Revolution. Autocratic regimes were losing the support of the people and demands for more democracy were on the rise. But the results were very different in France.

While the American Revolution had broad popular support, the use of violence and executions during the French Revolution had a chilling effect. After the Revolution ran its course, the French turned to a military figure,

Napoleon Bonaparte, who imposed yet another autocratic rule — one with secret police, a very nasty system of penal colonies, and terrible conditions for prisoners. For twenty-five years continental Europe was involved in almost continuous warfare until the final defeat of the French in Belgium at Waterloo in 1815.

After these wars, the consensus of many in power was that the popular "dream of democracy" was the cause of this social chaos. From the English general, the Duke of Wellington (known as the Iron Duke by the British people), to Metternich of Austria, those in power across Europe turned to repression to halt rebellion.

Meanwhile living conditions worsened in Britain and western and northern Europe as industrialization began to quicken after the Napoleonic Wars. Workers — men, women, and children — flooded into the cities to find work in the factories and mills. Twelve- to fourteen-hour days, six days a week was the norm. Heavy physical labour broke the spirits of workers. Accidents — even deaths — were seen as a cost of production. During the periodic bouts of economic depression, workers faced starvation. Emerging trade unions, formed to try and protect workers, were outlawed; strikes were often brutally put down by the army.

In Britain, conditions bordered on rebellion during times of depression in the nineteenth century. In August 1819, sixty thousand to eighty thousand people gathered in Manchester to listen to a popular reform speaker who advocated universal suffrage. The army attacked the crowd and eleven people were killed. Workers called it the Peterloo Massacre to satirize the Iron Duke, who was responsible for the attack. From 1830 to 1832 there were massive demonstrations supporting a reform bill going through Parliament. Some say that Britain has never been as close to revolution.[2]

In 1848–49, much of central Europe was on the brink of revolution and again it was dissatisfaction with the autocratic political structure that sparked the uprising. The movement was split between middle-class liberals who supported democratic reforms, individual rights, and the attempt to unify various German states, and working-class labourers and craftsmen who were protesting working and living conditions.

The uprisings in the German states were inspired by a revolt in Paris in 1848, which resulted in the abdication of the French king. Demonstrations spread to Austria and then to small German principalities. Each one had a different set of events, but repression was common in all of them. In Prussia hundreds were killed when the army attacked demonstrators. Ultimately the two elements of the uprising split and that gave the autocratic elements the ability to use force to crush the uprising.

One of the results of the uprising and repression of this movement was a massive migration of Germans to the United States. It is estimated that five million German-speaking people took the transatlantic trip and settled mainly in the American Midwest and Texas.

Largely unnoticed at the time were the activities of Karl Marx and Friedrich Engels in these uprisings. Shortly afterwards they wrote *The Communist Manifesto,* their reflections on these events. Their commitment to revolution came out of their belief that the political and economic system could not be reformed and only revolution could lead to the needed social and political change. Repression, they believed, would lead to revolt and ultimately a communist society.

Following the book's publication in 1849, Marx fled to London, where he lived and worked for the rest of his life. The *Manifesto*, and other works of Marx and Engels, shaped world history for much of the twentieth century and are influential even to this day.

* * *

REVOLT IN THE CANADAS

These complicated series of events and ideas are the context that shaped the political unrest of Upper and Lower Canada in the early part of the nineteenth century. Democracy was in the air, seeded by the Enlightenment philosophers. The Americans, enemies of the British in the War of 1812, were developing a vibrant democracy in their territory just to the south. But Upper and Lower Canada were colonies governed by British administrators who came from aristocratic social circles in the mother country and were obsessed with concerns about rebellion and insurrection. The people of both Canadas chafed under their repressive British governors.

Upper Canada's first lieutenant governor, Lord Simcoe, was an aristocrat who wanted to develop a colony, not unlike Britain at the time, of an established elite leading a country made up of farmers and artisans — but coming into the country were more and more American settlers looking for inexpensive, fertile land. They brought their republican ideas with them.

After Simcoe, a series of British lieutenant governors who had patronage connections to the British government were appointed. A small group of officials and their supporters emerged around the lieutenant governor and came to be called the Family Compact. This was a group linked to the professional and mercantile classes centred on the capital that supported the British and the established church.

In Lower Canada the social and political situation was even more polarized. The vast majority of the population was French Canadian farmers who were Catholic, unlike the Protestant population in Upper Canada. Around the lieutenant governor emerged a small group of English-speaking merchants, businessmen, and professionals that came to be called the Château Clique. They used their power and influence to further their interests by aggressively pursuing canal building and promoting banks. The polarization between these two groups was focused on the legislative assembly that was dominated by the emerging French middle class, led by Louis-Joseph Papineau.[3]

Finally in 1837 rebellion broke out in both Upper and Lower Canada. In Toronto on December 7 a group of about four hundred rebels, composed mainly of farmers and artisans, marched down Yonge Street. They were met by a larger number of royalists. Shots were exchanged and the rebels scattered. William Lyon Mackenzie, the leader of the revolt, and others fled to the United States and the rebellion collapsed. Two of the rebels were hanged for their role in the uprising.[4]

In Lower Canada the rebellion was a much more serious challenge to British rule. The polarization between the French Patriots, as they were called, and the English elite, the Château Clique, came to a head in the Assembly, dominated by the Patriots, in 1834. The Patriots passed ninety-two resolutions that contained their grievances and sent them to London. The most important contained their demand for responsible, or democratic, government, which would make the executive committee responsible to the elected Assembly. The British government ignored the demands. In Lower Canada the agitation for rebellion grew and ethnic divisions became more intense.

In 1837 London finally responded to the ninety-two resolutions by rejecting the major demands. In response, the Patriots organized a boycott of British goods. The British brought in regular troops. Agitation broke out and by November there were armed skirmishes. There was fierce resistance by the Patriots. More skirmishes happened. The British burned villages and homes, and looting took place, but the rebellion collapsed. A year later, in November 1838, a second insurgency broke out, but it soon collapsed as well.

The result was more repression. The leaders fled. Papineau settled in France. Hundreds of Patriots were wounded and hundreds more imprisoned. In total there were 325 killed, 27 of them soldiers. Ultimately 108 men were convicted; 99 were condemned to death, but only 12 went to the gallows, and 58 were transported to Australia.

The most important consequences of the two uprisings were political. A more liberal government had been elected in Britain, and they sent Lord Durham to investigate. His recommendations were to unite Upper and Lower Canada into one colony. This was something that the Montreal English elite had long advocated, but the French opposed because they feared their political influence would be swamped by the English votes of Upper Canada, a fear that soon proved to be real. But in the process, responsible government was granted.

Canadians are often reminded that we are a country of "peace, order, and good government," but our democracy was forged in the process of insurrection and rebellion. We followed a similar pattern of other countries in this turbulent era.

* * *

ELITES AND POLITICS

Autocratic governments led by kings, queens, dictators, and authoritarian strongmen all have one thing in common: they are supported by elites who benefit economically and socially by giving their support to the regime. It is a reciprocal relationship. The government is strengthened by their support, and in turn, they receive benefits of wealth and prestige.

This was true in the days of the absolute monarchs, and it continues in the dictatorships of the present. We can even see it operating in Canada before the establishment of responsible government. Members of the Family Compact and the Château Clique received rich rewards, and that was the main reason they supported the inept and out of touch colonial governments.

This fundamental grievance is why revolts and revolution have been so common in the last 250 years. The reason for such clashes has often been less a struggle for democracy than anger on the part of ordinary people at a political and social system that gives rich rewards to small groups for their loyalty to autocratic governments. The people are willing to struggle, and even put their lives on the line, in order to establish a system of government that promises equality for all.

By 1840 representative democracy had emerged in the two Canadas and in the Maritime colonies, but did it lead to equality for all? As we will see, this form of government led to a new elite — not the clique surrounding the governor, but a powerful business elite.

CHAPTER 2

ELECTIONS AND UNIVERSAL SUFFRAGE

Canadians are taught that we have had a democratic country since the 1840s, when responsible government was established, but if you judge democracy by the right to vote and participate in our democratic processes, ours was a very limited democracy until relatively recently. Incredible as it sounds, it was not until 1960 that the country truly had universal suffrage. Today the only people living in Canada who do not have the right to vote are non-citizens and those under eighteen years of age, but this was not always the case.

It is tempting to explain why groups did not have full citizens' rights by saying that they were perceived by the elite as being a threat to the status quo. That is partly true, but the main reason was prejudice against minority groups that was shared by many Canadians. However, the elite gained real advantages from a restricted franchise.

* * *

PROPERTY QUALIFICATIONS

In the election of 1867, the year of Confederation, only 361,028 people out of a population of 3.5 million had the right to vote. That is little more than one in ten. People were disqualified because they were women, minors, aboriginals, minority groups, or because they did not meet the property qualifications. By today's standards, Canada could hardly be considered democratic at all.

There was a deep and abiding prejudice against the poor and working people in the nineteenth century and the early decades of the twentieth. It was felt that they did not have enough education, information, or intelligence to participate in politics and exercise democratic responsibilities. Some worried they were prone to radical and revolutionary opinions. That prejudice conjured up the notion that, if given the vote, the poor would use it to take the property of the rich, reason enough to deny them the vote.[1]

Protecting the wealth of the affluent by denying the vote to those without property was practised in virtually all European countries at the time. In the United States, as we have seen, fear of the lower classes was an important theme in the debate around the Constitution. Most states denied the vote to those without property in the early decades of the republic, but by 1856 property qualifications were eliminated in the United States, and all white men were allowed to vote.

A few years after the Civil War, in 1870, the franchise was extended to blacks, but it was not long before segregationists in the American South found ways to deny blacks the vote using qualifications like poll taxes and literacy tests. It was not until the Voting Rights Act of 1965 that discrimination on the basis of race and ethnicity was finally eliminated in the United States.

In Great Britain, the other country that English-speaking Canadians looked to as a model, property qualifications to vote were a major political issue until well into the twentieth century. Restrictions of the franchise only intensified the conflict between the classes. By the 1830s the Chartist Movement emerged to demand universal male suffrage, but still it took decades to achieve. By 1867 working men in urban areas of Britain had the vote, but it was not until 1918 that universal male suffrage with no property qualifications was legislated. This was only after hundreds of thousands of working men and women had lost their lives fighting for Britain in the Great War. It was not until 1928 that all women got the vote.

In the first decades after Confederation, qualifications to vote were set by the provinces. All of them had property qualifications to vote, but they varied greatly. In 1885 the federal government passed the Electoral Franchise Act, setting who was qualified to vote. An elector had to be male, twenty-one years of age or older, a British subject by birth or naturalization, and own property worth $300 in cities, $200 in towns, or $150 in rural areas. At that time most manual workers did not own property and were unable to vote.

Both British Columbia and Prince Edward Island had universal male suffrage and no property qualifications before 1885. The legislation allowed them to retain that practice. In B.C., however, people from the Orient were not allowed to vote. There was massive prejudice against the Chinese and Japanese. Riots led to the smashing of their shops and other racist attacks. Immigration of people from the Orient was severely restricted. Even Prime Minister John A. Macdonald reflected these attitudes. He said that persons of the Mongolian and Chinese races should not have the right to vote because they had "no British instincts, or British feelings, or aspirations."[2] The Electoral Franchise Act of 1885 denied them the vote across Canada.

Nineteenth-century Canadian elections were marked by massive electoral fraud. Except in New Brunswick, there was no secret ballot for the first two federal elections. Voters cast their ballot orally. This led to intimidation. Elections were held on different days in different parts of the country. A candidate defeated in one riding could move to another. Both of these practices were changed after the Liberals were elected in 1874, but other problems continued.

On voter lists there were names of people who were long dead, and yet somehow they rose from their graves on Election Day in order to vote. Money flowed and the buying of votes was widespread. In the Maritimes a bottle of rum was the cost of a vote, and in much of the rest of the country a proper vote resulted in jobs or special favours. Scores of riding contests were held to be invalid because of various frauds, and yet the corruption went on from election to election.

Property qualifications to vote continued well into the twentieth century in some provinces. Finally, by 1920, they were eliminated. However, many municipalities required voters to own property until after the Second World War. This was justified with the argument that property tax, the main source of revenue for municipalities, was paid only by property owners. It ignored the fact that tenants paid property taxes indirectly when they paid their rent.

* * *

WOMEN AND THE VOTE

If prejudice was the reason used to deny the vote to workers or people from the Orient, it was also used to deny the vote to women. In the nineteenth century women were expected to be homemakers and tend the children. The affairs of state were believed to be the preserve of men. This was the middle-class ideal but in practice many women worked out of the home in factories and farms.

As the century went on women played more and more of an active role in the affairs of the nation and began to demand the vote. The majority of men opposed this extension of the franchise, claiming that it was not appropriate for women to be involved in messy politics with its compromises and backroom deals. By the end of the century, granting women the right to vote had become one of the major political issues of the day.

Before Confederation there were examples of women having the right to vote. This was particularly true in Lower Canada and parts of the Maritimes. Gradually, however, women lost the right to vote. By 1867 they were denied the right to vote across the country.

In the decade after Confederation the movement for women's suffrage had appeared in all of the English-speaking provinces. This was not true in French-speaking Quebec. The conservatism of the Catholic Church discouraged the involvement of women in politics. Ontario was a leading centre for women's suffrage in the 1870s. The Toronto Literary Club was established in 1876 by Dr. Emily Stowe, Canada's first female doctor. Founded to promote women's suffrage, the club attracted many of the city's professional women. In 1883 it changed its name to the Toronto Women's Suffrage Association.

By the last two decades of the nineteenth century suffragettes were involved not only in the demand for votes for women, but a broad social agenda that "embraced workplace safety, public health, child labour, prohibition of the production of and sale of alcohol, prostitution, the Canadianizing of immigrants as well as the vote for women."[3] The Women's Christian Temperance Union had emerged as one of the most powerful women's groups by this time. Virtually all of the leading Canadian suffragettes were members of the WCTU.

In the first decade of the twentieth century the women's movement had become a powerful movement of social reform, but central to their demand was the right to vote. However, politics was still the preserve of older, professional, wealthy men, who were conservative on social issues. Many women were convinced that they had to be able to vote if they were ever to bring about needed social reforms. Every year supporters of the suffragettes would table bills in provincial legislatures granting women the right to vote, and every year the proposed legislation was scorned and laughed at by the elected members before being defeated.

Across the English-speaking world, the demand for women's suffrage was growing. In Britain and the United States militant women were taking the lead, but different tactics were used in this country. In western Canada women used ridicule. Nellie McClung, a novelist and leading suffragette, produced a play in January 1914 in Winnipeg. It featured women playing the role of legislators, with men petitioning the government for the vote. McClung played the role of the premier. She mimicked then premier Rodmond Roblin, saying, "Man is made for higher and better things than voting. Men were made to support families. What is a home without a bank account?" Night after night the theatre was sold out, and the laughter, no doubt, could be heard all the way to the legislature building.

It was during the First World War (1914–18) that women finally got the vote. By then women were making a major contribution to the war effort, working in factories and tending the wounded on the battlefield, in hospitals, and at home. It began with the provinces. Manitoba granted women the vote in January 1916, Saskatchewan and Alberta a few months later, Ontario in February 1917, and British Columbia in April that year.

At the federal level, Robert Borden, the Conservative prime minister, faced a major problem. In Ontario and the Western provinces both men and women could vote, but in Quebec and the Maritimes only men could vote. The provinces made up the voter list. How could this be reconciled? But the real political problem Borden faced at the time was conscription. English-speaking Canada supported conscription, but in Quebec it was strongly opposed.

In an effort to strengthen the pro-conscription side, Borden passed legislation to give those in the military under the age of twenty-one the right to vote. This inadvertently gave nurses in the military the right to vote. They became the first women to vote in a federal election.

Shortly after, the Conservative government passed the War Time Elections Act, which gave the vote to female relatives of people serving in the military. This was an obvious attempt to inflate the vote of those who were in favour of conscription. Then, on March 21, 1918, Parliament passed a law providing universal female suffrage. Women had finally won the vote across Canada.

In 1920 yet another law was passed by Parliament; it gave universal access to the vote. Property qualifications were eliminated, and age and citizenship remained the major criteria for the right to vote. In the 1921 general election, Agnes Macphail was elected as the first female member of Parliament.

The Province of Quebec remained the last holdout against women's suffrage. In that province women got the right to vote in federal elections in 1918, like others across the country, but it was not until 1940 that provincial legislation was changed to allow women to vote in Quebec provincial elections.

It has taken a long time for women to be accepted in Canadian politics, but today it is finally happening. By 2015 the premiers of three of the largest provinces — Ontario, British Columbia, and Alberta — were women. Eighty-eight women were elected to the House of Commons, 26 percent of the House. A total of fifteen women were appointed to the Cabinet. Prime Minister Justin Trudeau famously said, when asked why he had given 50 percent of the cabinet positions to women, "Because it is 2015."

* * *

ALIENS AND INDIANS

To say that all adult citizens of Canada had the right to vote in federal elections in 1918 is not quite true. "Aliens," the term used for minority groups at the time, were denied the vote on racial and religious grounds. First Nations living on reserves were also denied the vote.

The Dominion Elections Act of 1920 declared that people disenfranchised by a province "for reasons of race" would also be excluded from the federal franchise. This was a concession to British Columbia, which had long denied the vote to people of Japanese and Chinese origin, as well as Hindus, Muslims, and Sikhs. Mennonites and Doukhobors were also excluded because they were conscientious objectors.

During the First World War there were a number of people from these groups who volunteered to serve in the Canadian Armed Forces. After the war there was a debate in Parliament during which members argued that these individuals had demonstrated their loyalty to the country, and the veterans should be given the vote, but that was defeated and the disenfranchisement continued. It was not until June 1948, after the Second World War, that this discrimination was ended.

The discrimination against First Nations people was even more blatant. Status Indians living on reserves were denied the vote. In the nineteenth century, if an adult male left the reserve, gave up his Indian status, and met all other criteria such as property qualifications, he would be given the vote, but that was a very small number of people. In 1885 status Indians in eastern Canada were given the right to vote but that was revoked in 1898.

This was a clear example of discrimination against First Nations people. It was said that they didn't have enough education, or that they would be overly influenced by others. Some argued that aboriginals did not want the vote. It is clear that they were not demanding the vote or mounting a public campaign for the vote, like suffragettes, but what the lack of the franchise did was deny native people any political influence in Canadian politics at any level for decades.

It was not until 1960 that First Nations people were granted the right to vote. John Diefenbaker led the fight. He had grown up on the Prairies and practised law there. He witnessed the discrimination against aboriginal people and was determined to do something about it. When Diefenbaker was prime minister the law was changed to grant all aboriginal people the right to vote.

Finally, in 1960, Canada could claim that it was a democratic country that granted the vote to all adult citizens regardless of gender, income, race, or religion.

* * *

FORGING A MORE REPRESENTATIVE DEMOCRACY

The theory of representative democracy is that we select the politicians who are to represent us through the process of elections. Those elected represent our views in Parliament or other democratic councils. That is the theory; the problem is that it does not work very well in Canada.

Our electoral system is called *first past the post*. A riding (constituency or ward) is drawn up by electoral officers and all citizens are eligible to stand for election. In federal and provincial elections, the candidates are usually from the active political parties. Today there are four: Liberal, Conservative, New Democratic, and Green. There can be others, too: Communist, Marxist-Leninist, Libertarian, Rhinoceros, and so on. In many municipal elections there are no political parties, and there are sometimes scores of independent candidates. It may be messy, and confusing, but that's democracy. All eligible voters have the right to stand for office.

The problem is that the first-past-the-post electoral system is a winner-takes-all system. The candidate with the most votes in an electoral district is elected and all others are defeated. That means that a candidate can win with much less than 50 percent of the votes in the riding. Some elections of candidates are won with 30 percent of the votes, or even less. What about those people who voted for losing candidates? Are their votes wasted? Some would say yes.

Compounding the problem is that, depending on the vote splits, political parties can win a majority in Parliament with much less than 50 percent of the vote. In fact, rarely has a political party gotten 50 percent of the vote in recent Canadian elections. In the 2015 election, the Liberals, led by Justin Trudeau, won 39.5 percent of the vote nationally, but won a majority government with over 50 percent of the seats in the House of Commons. That is not unusual. In the 2011 election, the Conservatives, led by Stephen Harper, won 39.6 percent of the vote nationally but won a majority government. Clearly the first-past-the-post system is not one in which the elected politicians are representative of the electorate, and that is what representative democracy is supposed to be all about.

This issue has been talked about for years and and there is a promise that we are on the brink of changing our electoral system. In the 2015 election Justin Trudeau promised that if the Liberals were elected it would be the last election using the first-past-the-post system. This was not the most important issue in the election, but it helped define the Liberals as seeking genuine reform. The promise was welcomed by supporters of the NDP and Green Party, who have long believed that they are underrepresented in parliament.

After the election, many urged the Liberals, now the government, to move ahead on electoral reform. That is when things became very messy. The

Conservatives prefer the existing first-past-the-post system and demanded that there be a referendum, arguing that this was a substantial change to our democratic system and must be supported by the majority of the people. Both the NDP and the Green Party prefer proportional representation, where the party standings in the House reflect the proportion of the votes received by the party across the country. The Liberals support a system of ranked ballots, where electors rank the parties according to their preference.

Obviously, each party was advocating electoral systems that would benefit them. To demonstrate the impact of each system, the Council of Canadians projected what they thought the party representation of the 338 seats in the House of Commons would be under the different electoral systems.

ELECTORAL SYSTEMS AND SEATS IN THE HOUSE OF COMMONS[4]

	2015 election result	2015 result with proportional	2015 result with ranked ballots
Liberal	184	134	224
Conservative	99	109	61
NDP	44	67	50
Bloc	10	16	2
Green	1	12	1
Total	338	338	338

It would be nice to think that people could intervene in this partisan debate and resolve the issue with a referendum, but don't expect that to happen. The history of referendums shows that they have become a convenient political tool to block change.

Will Justin Trudeau deliver on his promise to change the electoral system? It will take a lot of political magic and good will to make that happen.

* * *

DEMOCRACY, THE VOTE, AND POLITICAL PROCESS

It took almost a century, but gradually the Canadian electoral system has grown more democratic, and even more significant reforms are on the horizon. Today all adult citizens have the vote, and with proportional representation our political system should reflect the political views of the entire population. Gradually, representative democracy has grown strong, and hopefully it will get even stronger in the near future.

And yet the history of the expansion of the franchise is not encouraging. Over time the corporate and wealthy elite have been increasing their political power and influence. The fear that the majority would use their electoral power to take from the wealthy is hardly true. In fact, as both left and right political thinkers have predicted, representative democracy has been a boon to capitalism and has contributed to inequality. The only conclusion is that, while important, the franchise is only one element of democracy.

As we will see, wealth and influence remain powerful forces in Canadian democracy.

CHAPTER 3

DEMOCRACY AND THE RISE OF CANADIAN CAPITALISM

To understand elite control in the period when Europeans first came to this continent all we need do is look at people's motivations for coming here: profit.

French traders came to Tadoussac, Quebec, where the Saguenay River empties into the St. Lawrence, in the year 1600 to trade in furs. In 1608 Samuel de Champlain established a more permanent base for the trade at Quebec. In 1614 the Dutch built a trading post at what is today Albany, New York. The competition for furs soon pitted native people against each other in a deadly contest to dominate the trade. In time, that competition developed into a series of wars between the English and French.

To exploit the fur trade and other resources, the French Crown established a monopoly in New France called the Compagnie des Cent-Associés (Company of One Hundred Associates). Soon the English replaced the Dutch in the New World. By 1665 they realized the advantage of the Hudson Bay route, thanks to the fur traders Pierre-Esprit Radisson and Médard Chouart des Groseilliers. In 1670 a royal charter was given to the Hudson's Bay Company, a group of wealthy English merchants who had close associations with King Charles II. This gave them monopoly control over Rupert's Land, and all of the land draining into Hudson Bay, about 15 percent of the total North American continent.

The parallels are striking. Both the French and the English simply took possession of the land in the name of the Crowns of their respective countries and granted the rights to exploit these lands to favourites of the king. Aboriginal people were assumed to have no rights, but they soon became the vital link in the fur trade. They collected and cured the furs, transported them over long distances to the trading posts, and received payment in trade goods like pots, knives, weapons, beads, and liquor. Meanwhile the real profits went to the traders and to the Crown. This structure in the fur trade remained until well into the twentieth century.

This type of economic and political system, in which the major rewards went to the wealthy and politically powerful, continues to this day, but it has changed considerably over time as a result of different ideologies and the strengthening of democracy in Canada. An exhaustive examination of the relationship between business and government would require volumes of text, but let's look at some examples at national, provincial, and local levels.

* * *

"RAILWAYS ARE MY POLITICS"

Once the British took over New France in 1759 the new government supported the British economic interests in the fur trade. As the economy changed, successive governments supported the merchants and industrialists with grants, subsidies in land and economic policies designed to promote and support business. Not surprisingly it was attempts to improve transportation system in this huge, isolated country that received most of the benefits. The justification was that better transportation would help to move goods to market and that was a broad benefit to all businesses.

Canals built by private companies were the first large infrastructure projects in this country. The Lachine Canal on Montreal Island was built in 1825 to bypass the Lachine Rapids; the Rideau Canal, a military project, was opened in 1826; the Welland Canal, linking Lakes Erie and Ontario, opened in 1829. Soon other canals bypassing smaller rapids on the St. Lawrence River were built, and some of the existing canals were expanded and improved.

It was not long before these canals were in financial difficulties and taken over by the government. A similar venture in Nova Scotia met the same fate. These were huge projects for that day, and it was the costs that drove the companies into bankruptcy and government ownership. That, in turn, led to higher taxes. This angered the French in Lower Canada. They believed, correctly as it turned out, that the prime beneficiaries of the canals would be the farmers and merchants of Upper Canada, because their costs to get grain to market were lowered. And yet the people of Lower Canada were forced to pay for the canals with higher taxes. This was an important grievance in the 1837 Patriots uprising in Lower Canada.[1]

Canals set the precedent for government support of private enterprise in Canada, but it was railways that took the system of subsidies to stratospheric levels. The Great Western Railway was not the first in Canada, but in time it became one of the most important.[2]

In 1834 a group of Hamilton, Ontario, businessmen received a charter from the legislature to build a railroad between Hamilton and London called the London and Gore Railroad. Soon it became apparent that the main stumbling block was raising sufficient capital. The only possibility was to tap the public purse to raise the funds.

The leader of this group was Sir Allan MacNab, a member of the legislature, businessman and member of the Family Compact. MacNab went on to become speaker of the legislature and for a short time was premier of Upper Canada. He was also chairman of the Legislative Assembly Standing Committee on Railways. The merging of his political and business activities was best expressed when he said, "Railways are my politics." He meant that literally. MacNab used his considerable political influence to promote his private business interests, namely his efforts to fund railways.

This was typical of the politics of that day, and it was aided and abetted by the restrictions of the franchise. As we have seen, at that time only adult male property owners had the right to vote. Women, aboriginals, farm labourers, and most artisans and workers could not vote. The Legislature, as a result, was dominated by merchants, financers, and other businessmen who saw nothing wrong with using the public treasury to promote and finance their own business interests.

By 1845 the London and Gore Railroad had been transformed into the Great Western Railway; MacNab was the president, and the proposed route was to go from Niagara Falls through Hamilton, Brantford, Woodstock, London, Chatham, and terminate in Windsor. It was promoted as a railway that would transport agricultural goods, particularly grain, from the fast-growing area of southwestern Ontario to the port of Hamilton. It was also touted as the shortest route between New York and Boston in the East to Chicago and the West.

But where were MacNab and his business associates going to get the money to build this massive project? First they tried the City of Hamilton, but even the prominence and influence of the promoters fell flat. Hamilton council voted only £25 for the railway. But the campaign was just beginning. Pamphlets and books extolling the benefits of railways were published. Outlandish claims of the new railway age were made, letters to the editor and editorials were written. Finally, this groundwork began to pay dividends.

In 1849 the Legislative Assembly of the Province of Canada passed a bill called the Guarantee Act. It was conceived by Francis Hincks, another railway entrepreneur, and supported by Sir Allan MacNab and others. It stated that the government would "lend to companies incorporated for the construction of railways not less than seventy-five miles in length, a sum sufficient to complete the road." By the time the Great Western was built, the Canadian government had loaned the company £770,000, a fantastic sum if converted to today's dollars.

This was just the beginning of the massive public subsidy program for railroads. Legislation forbade municipalities from buying stock in private companies, but Hincks and MacNab soon changed that by amending the legislation. Hamilton voted to purchase £100,000 of Great Western stock. Local people were up in arms and the stock purchase was reduced to £50,000, still a staggering amount of money for a small frontier city. All along the railway line municipalities bought stock in the company, donated land, or provided other forms of subsidies.

The Great Western was the first railroad to take advantage of government subsidies; it was soon followed, however, by the Grand Trunk Railroad, which was an even more elaborate railway scheme. This company was first incorporated in 1852 to build a railroad between Montreal and Toronto, the two largest cities in the country. The finances came from the Legislative Assembly via the Guarantee Act, municipalities who gave both money and land, and investors from Great Britain who were attracted by the government subsidies and guarantees.

By 1856 the line between Toronto and Montreal was completed and in that same year a line between Toronto and Sarnia was opened to capture trade to Chicago and further west. The company also built a line between Montreal and Riviere-du-Loup and another to Portland, Maine, giving the

Grand Trunk year-round saltwater access. At that time the railroad was the largest in the world with 1,277 miles (2,055 km) of track.

By the 1860s Canadians had become convinced that railways were essential for the development of the country. In 1867 Canada was formed as a country with the union of Ontario, Quebec, New Brunswick, and Nova Scotia. It is unlikely that the two Maritime provinces would have agreed to the union without the promise to build a railway to Halifax. It took a decade to complete, but the Intercolonial Railway to the Maritime provinces, as it was called, was built and financed entirely by the Canadian government. However, it remained in private hands.

All of these railways soon were in financial difficulty. Despite the hype and the subsidies none of them made money. In 1882 the Great Western was near bankruptcy and was absorbed by the Grand Trunk. But even the tottering financial structure of the industry did not deter other railway promotions.

To attract British Columbia into the Canadian Confederation, the country promised to build a transcontinental railway across the continent. What is surprising is that in spite of enormous geographical hurdles, political controversies, and financial problems, the Canadian Pacific Railway (CPR) actually became a reality. The secret was the financial subsidies to the company on a scale that has never been surpassed in our history. In total the CPR received $63.5 million in public funds, $35 million in government loans, 10.4 million hectares of prime farmland on the prairies, tax emptions for CPR property, and a guaranteed monopoly until 1900. Finally, with all of this largesse, Canada had a railway that was profitable.

It was not until the 1920s that the railway craze finally came to an end in Canada. Two more transcontinental railways were built to the west coast before it became obvious that the country had too many railroads and tracks for a country with a small population. In 1923 the Grand Trunk and other railways were nationalized and reorganized into the Canadian National Railways. Since then Canada has had two transcontinental railways, and today they both are profitable. Historians agree that despite all of the public money and all the political problems, railways have made a major contribution to the prosperity of this country.

* * *

THE NATIONAL POLICY

At this late date it is impossible to tell what most Canadians at the time felt about the massive subsidy system for railways. Clearly it would never have happened without the control of the legislature by business interests. But in time people came to like the convenience the railways delivered, the ease in transportation, and the cheaper goods that came from lower transportation costs. Many, no doubt, were outraged at the level of subsidies given to private interests, but others thought that if the price to be paid for a better transportation system was government subsidies, then so be it.

By the middle and end of the nineteenth century there were two divergent political strategies governments were using to bring "progress" (*economic development* as we call it today). Britain was the leading industrial country at that time, and had adopted a system of free trade. They benefited enormously from this system because they had a high level of industrial development, and long-standing trading relationships with their colonies and other countries. Britain exported goods around the world; London was the major financial capital at that time; and the wealthy reaped huge profits from their investments in the colonies, particularly India, and other developing countries, including Canada.

The United States, by contrast, developed a dynamic economic system with a policy of protectionism supported by high tariffs of 35 percent to keep out foreign imports. They also paid for their railways with government grants and free land in much the same way as was done in Canada. By the post–Civil War period the Americans had a market protected from foreign competition by high tariffs, a large and growing population, and an extensive system of railways, canals, and shipping. As a consequence, the United States went through a period of unprecedented economic takeoff.

Canadians wanted to become a modern, developed society just like the Americans and the British, but it was more difficult here. Canada was then and remains a vast country with a small population. How could it industrialize, and where was the money going to come from? The person who understood this more clearly than anyone was the wiliest and most gifted politician Canada produced in the nineteenth century: John A. Macdonald.

The question was, should Canada adopt free trade, like Britain — the "mother country" — or should it follow the lead of the United States by creating a protected market? The issue was resolved in the hotly contested election of

1878. The Liberals were free traders. The ideology of liberalism in both Britain and Canada at that time was support of individual rights, non-interference of government in the affairs of business, and free trade. The Conservatives, led by John A. Macdonald, advocated high tariffs to protect and stimulate industry.

The country was divided on this issue, as were the political parties. Most, but certainly not all manufacturers and their workers supported protectionism. The base of Conservative support was the large cities of Montreal, Toronto, and Hamilton. Farmers (about half the people in the country lived either on farms or small towns at that time) tended to support free trade because it meant lower costs for manufactured goods like farm equipment. After a hard-fought election Macdonald and his Conservatives won, and in 1879 they legislated high tariffs, dressing it up as the National Policy.

Was the National Policy a subsidy to business? Yes. There can be no doubt about that. It meant higher prices for Canadians, and a protected, subsidized market. Canadian business interests, particularly manufacturers, benefited from this policy. It led to the formation of many firms that would have been uncompetitive if they were in another market, but Canadians knew all that during the election, and they still chose protectionism. It was a democratic choice made by the people.

Free trade versus protectionism remains a central issue in Canadian politics that has returned in different forms until today. The federal election of 1911 was fought on precisely this issue. The Liberals, led by Wilfrid Laurier, supported free trade with the United States while the Conservatives, under Robert Borden, opposed it. The Conservatives won with 132 seats to the Liberals' 85.

The 1988 election again saw free trade as the central issue of the campaign, but this time the party positions were reversed. Brian Mulroney's Progressive Conservatives advocated free trade with the United States under the North American Free Trade Agreement, while both the Liberals and the New Democrats opposed it. The Conservatives won the election and the agreement was implemented.

Since that time both Conservatives and Liberals have supported free trade and a number of trade agreements have been signed, but there is still deep opposition in some quarters of the country. Many workers and trade unions oppose increasing free trade because they see it as eroding jobs and reducing their incomes. This issue promises to be with us for years to come.

* * *

MUNICIPAL SUBSIDIES

Let's come back to the issue that we have been discussing, namely, the system of subsidies to business in this country. What happened in the years leading up to the First World War was the establishment of a municipal subsidy system that came close to bankrupting many of our cities. It would be difficult to describe the full extent of these subsidies because it was so extensive, but the giveaways in the city of Hamilton, Ontario, are more than enough to illustrate what was going on across Canada and the continent.[3]

Hamilton, and the owners and workers in its factories, mills, and foundries, benefited from the railway boom. By the middle of the nineteenth century the city had established an industrial base and strongly supported protectionism. During the 1878 election John A. Macdonald gave a speech in the city and made the following statement, "Let each manufacturer tell us what he wants and we will try and give him what he needs."[4] He would not have dared to make a statement like that in other parts of the country, but in Hamilton there was strong support for subsidizing industry.

After the National Policy was enacted Hamilton's industries boomed. Its foundries supplied the railways and made stoves for farmhouses and tools for labourers. There were textile mills, tobacco factories, and canneries. Stevedores were busy on the waterfront, and every day teams of workers loaded freight cars with goods. Hamiltonians understood that their future was tied to industry and adopted the motto "The Ambitious City."

By the end of the century the city's political leaders decided to attract even more companies with subsidies, lots of them. In 1890 the city's finance committee "recommended that all manufacturers locating in the city should be exempted from paying taxes for ten years on all of their buildings, machinery, tools, income, and personal property."[5] The motion failed at city council, but it signalled what was to become a vast outpouring of subsidies for companies willing to locate in Hamilton.

In 1893 the first grants were given to the steel industry. A group of New York businessmen were given a free site of seventy-five acres of land and promised a bonus of $100,000 if a $400,000 blast furnace and a $400,000 open hearth mill were built and running by 1894.[6] The land was valued at

$35,000 at the time. It was a local beauty spot called Huckleberry Point on the edge of Hamilton Harbour. The site soon became the centre of the massive installations that after 1910 became the Steel Company of Canada, or Stelco.

In the 1890s the bylaws of Hamilton were filled with special tax concessions and bonuses paid out to companies locating in the city. It was only after the turn of the century that the subsidies became truly enormous. In 1897 Westinghouse located in the city and in 1903 an inducement was given to the company that stated, "The taxes … on all property existing or thereafter established were fixed at $1,500 per annum for 1905 to 1909, $3,000 from 1910 to 1914, and $4,500 from 1915 to 1919."[7]

In 1902 Hamilton City Council agreed to pay the Deering Agricultural Implement Company $50,000 if they located in the city. This agreement had to be ratified by the majority of voters in a city-wide referendum. It was expected it would be accepted because it was much like subsidies that were given to other companies. Instead, the motion was rejected by a large margin. Why? Deering was anti-union. In Illinois it ran an *open shop*, meaning that workers could not be forced to join a union. The growing trade union movement in Hamilton used Deering's anti-union history to campaign against the agreement.

But this was not the end of the matter. Deering was invited back to the city, and an even more inviting proposal was made to them. The city agreed to annex a large block of land that included the site Deering had selected for its plant. They also agreed that the land would be assessed as farmland in 1903, and that valuation would prevail for the next twenty years. This agreement did not have to be ratified by a referendum and was passed by city council. In total over the next twenty years this subsidy amounted to far more than the original offer of $50,000.[8]

Within a short period of time, that slice of land annexed by the city to subsidize Deering, became the centre of industrial development in Hamilton. Even today, more than one hundred years later, it remains among the most heavily industrialized pieces of land in Canada. After the bylaw was passed all companies locating in the area were to be taxed as farmland at the old Barton Township rate for fifteen years.[9]

It is difficult to calculate the extent of the city's subsidy program at this time because of the complicated tax concessions, but it was massive. By the early 1920s the Ontario government became so alarmed at the level of subsidies given to businesses by municipalities that they feared some may face a financial crisis. Finally, these concessions to business were stopped altogether with provincial legislation.

David Russell, who studied the system of subsidies in the 1930s not long after the program was killed, concluded that the giveaways were so generous it is likely the companies never paid for the city services that they received during that time. He wrote, "Whether the inequalities of such a system placed a burden upon the tax payer of the city exceeding the benefits received, is more than a debatable question."[10]

Hamilton's system of municipal subsidies is only a small example of hand-outs to business. Across Canada and the United States incentives in the form of money, gifts of land, and tax breaks flowed. The practice was killed in Ontario but in parts of the United States municipal subsidy programs continue unabated.

* * *

LAISSEZ-FAIRE, SOCIALISM, AND PRAGMATISM

The period between the two wars was a time of intense political polarization between left and right in Canada. It began with the Winnipeg General Strike in 1919 and continued with labour and social strife throughout the era. The economic forces that shaped the period were the wild ride of the stock market in the 1920s, the crash of October 1929, and the Depression of the 1930s, which lasted ten long, desperate years.

Laissez-faire economic policies were in ascendency during the period at both federal and provincial levels, and those policies advocated balanced budgets and government non-interference in business. This contributed to drift and lack of direction. High tariffs on manufactured products remained in place. Industry serviced the Canadian market. Subsidy programs were much reduced. There were some exports of agricultural products and natural resources, but the economy languished.

One industry that did thrive was the liquor business. Prohibition on the sale of booze was legislated federally during the First World War as part of the war effort. This was lifted after the war and the regulation of alcohol became a provincial responsibility. Quebec quickly made the liquor trade legal. Ontario and the rest of the country kept consumption of liquor illegal but allowed it to be manufactured.

In the United States the Constitution was amended to ban the manufacture and consumption of alcohol. The amendment, known as the Volstead Act, was passed in 1919. It remained in force until 1933 when it was finally rescinded. A suddenly dry but enormously thirsty neighbour to the south created a perfect opportunity for Canadian distilleries and breweries. They could manufacture all of the alcohol they wanted as long as it was for export, and the illegal market south of the border was insatiable. For those bold enough to be bootleggers, the profits were substantial. Good times returned to places like Windsor, Ontario, and Moose Jaw, Saskatchewan. Border towns from Vancouver Island to Nova Scotia became boomtowns.

In the Depression the economy shrank dramatically, and unemployment reached 30 percent or more by 1933. R.B. Bennett and the Conservatives came to power in 1930. Their belief in laissez-faire led them to do little or nothing to solve the worst economic crisis that has ever faced the county. Their only response to unemployment was to establish work camps for single, unemployed men. Agitation increased, and so did repression by the police.

By 1935 Bennett realized that something drastic had to be done. He announced Canada's New Deal, following the Roosevelt program, but by then it was too late. Mackenzie King and the Liberals were re-elected but social conditions changed very little until war broke out in 1939.

It was the Second World War that changed Canada's economic policies forever. The federal government put the country on a war footing and virtually took over the Canadian economy. This time it was not a system of subsidies for business. Companies were told what to produce and what prices they were to receive. The companies stayed in private hands, but control was in the hands of the federal government.

Canada's achievements on the home front were remarkable. The economy rebounded and prosperity quickly returned. This demonstrated the power of government to mobilize the economy in the face of crisis. The first casualty of the war was laissez-faire. Socialism fared better, but the real victor was pragmatism: do what is necessary.

* * *

CORPORATE WELFARE

After the Second World War, Canada was in a very enviable position. Casualties in the war were light in comparison to other countries, our industries were undamaged, and the labour force was relatively young and well educated. Government had learned to control the wild swings of the economy, thanks to Keynesianism, and careful attention to details like interest rates.

Although few cared to admit it in case Canada was seen to be a socialist country, we had developed a mixed economy, with most enterprises in private hands and strong, interventionist governments willing to use their power to regulate business. The largest and most profitable sectors of the economy were dominated by corporations that had near monopolistic control over their markets. Governments — federal, provincial, and municipal — delivered infrastructure like roads, water, expressways, harbours, canals, and major airports. They owned vital utilities and services like Ontario Hydro, the St. Lawrence Seaway, Trans-Canada Airlines (later Air Canada), and CN Rail.

The welfare state was legislated and improved: old age pensions, worker's compensation, social assistance, and the most important program of all, comprehensive Canada-wide Medicare, was introduced in 1961. At the same time governments resumed their practice of subsidizing private companies.

In 1972 David Lewis, the then leader of the NDP, published the book *Louder Voices: The Corporate Welfare Bums*. He argued that it was not the poor who exploited government or who were the welfare bums in the country; it was the large corporations. Lewis showed how millions of dollars of government subsidies were going to wealthy companies like the Aluminum Company of Canada, Canadian Westinghouse, and the Michelin tire company. Later he added Shell Canada, Denison Mines, Dofasco, Falconbridge, Bell Canada, and many more.

From the 1970s to today corporate welfare has grown to become one of the biggest, and most expensive, government programs in the country, involving all three levels of government: federal, provincial, and municipal. In 2014 Mark Milke, an independent business analyst based in Calgary, did a study of all of the corporate subsidies given out in the country. He found that between 1981 and 2009 the federal government spent $343 billion to subsidize private corporations, government businesses, and consumers. Provinces collectively spent $287 billion, and municipalities $54 billion. This totals a whopping $684 billion.[11]

Over this twenty-eight-year period, Quebec had the highest level of subsidies at $115.5 billion. Ontario, with the largest population, spent $46.7 billion and Alberta $49.9 billion. In Alberta most of the $50 billion was spent in the seventies and eighties by the Peter Lougheed government in an attempt to diversify the Alberta economy. Claiming that much of the money had been wasted, Premier Ralph Klein cancelled the spending binge after being elected in 1992.

Not all corporations have benefited from government subsidies. Few grants went to small companies. Large food and retail corporations receive no, or very little, government help. It has been manufacturers who have received the lion's share of the money. This despite the fact that manufacturing in Canada has been declining relative to other industries. Today only about 11 percent of Canada's GDP comes from manufacturing.

The largest industry receiving subsidies has been the airlines. Bombardier has received over $1.1 billion since 1966 in grants, loan guarantees, and other programs. In 2015 they received $1 billion from the Quebec government and they have asked for another billion from the federal government. But they did not receive the largest subsidies of companies in the aviation sector. Pratt & Whitney, the engine manufacturer, received $3.3 billion. Airline manufacturers have tried to justify the level of subsidies they have received by saying that countries like the United States and Brazil also subsidize their aircraft manufacturers.

To complicate things, the competition to attract business has become international. Canada and the provinces often compete against low wage jurisdictions in the southern United States and Mexico. In the United States municipalities often bid up the amount of the subsidies they are willing to give in order to attract a manufacturer. Canada frequently loses out in this competition not only because they are not willing to put as much money and other benefits on the table, but also because this country has higher wages than Mexico and the southern states.

The film industry in Canada in recent years has benefited from the system of corporate subsidies. American production companies come to shoot in Canada because of the low Canadian dollar and to benefit from the system of tax credits, loans, and grants. Pixar Animation Studios, a subsidiary of the Walt Disney Company, located in Vancouver in 2010 to take advantage of a B.C. program of tax breaks for digital firms and animation, but in fall 2015 they closed up shop and moved back to California. This despite the fact that Disney made $1.6 billion in profits that year.[12]

This system of subsidies is rife with problems. Often what happens is that a company will receive subsidies to open a new plant, but at the same time they close another. Kellogg, for example, received a subsidy from the Ontario government to open a plant in eastern Ontario, but soon after it opened, the company shut down an older plant in London, Ontario. Mark Milke points out that many subsidies only redistribute jobs from one community to another. They do not create new jobs.[13]

Another problem is that governments and politicians are put in the position of judging the economic viability of companies — choosing winners and losers, in other words — and they are not very good at it. Ontario gave $7 million to a company called Global Sticks to locate in Thunder Bay. Global Sticks employed 130 people and made popsicle sticks and tongue depressors. They went bankrupt in 2012, owing $15 million.[14]

The system of government subsidies has become so prevalent and widespread today that there are businesses who spend much of their time trolling for public money, going from government to government, looking for subsidies and playing one government against another. Is it fraud? Probably not, but it is unlikely that these types of businesses will benefit the communities where they locate, or the workers that they hire.

Governments are under tremendous pressure to produce jobs, especially well-paying industrial jobs. This is particularly true today because manufacturing jobs are threatened and manual and semi-skilled jobs are disappearing. The politicians know that if they can attract new jobs or save plants from closing, the benefits in higher tax revenue and improved standards of living will be enormous. That is the justification, but more and more people on both the political left and right are questioning this. Mark Milke says the benefits are dubious at best. Others have pointed out that the $684 billion of corporate subsidies given by governments is about the same as the federal debt. Wouldn't Canada have been better off financially if that money had been used to pay the debt rather than to give subsidies to companies that are already profitable?

A recent study by the International Monetary Fund projected that energy subsidies worldwide were $5.3 trillion in 2015. Eliminating subsidies, they said, would reduce greenhouse gas emissions by 13 percent. They also pegged Canada's fossil fuel subsidies at $34 billion.[15] These figures not only included things like subsidies, but also what economists call *externalized costs*, like oil spills, traffic accidents, carbon emissions, air pollution, and road congestion.

That is a staggering amount of money, totalling 6.5 percent of global GDP. It may not be justified. How can you consider traffic accidents and road congestion as a subsidy to fossil fuel producers? But it does reflect the cost of corporate subsidies and suggests that it is time for a complete re-evaluation of the whole system of corporate welfare.

* * *

SOMETHING IS OUT OF WHACK

Something has gone very wrong in the political and economic system that we have created. The Enlightenment philosophers who dreamt of the benefits of democracy would be horrified at the way politics has become distorted to favour the wealthy and not the great majority of people.

Karl Marx, the most devastating critic of capitalism, said the "rich get richer and the poor get poorer" under capitalism. Most Canadians have not fallen into poverty, but the wealthy — the "1 percent" as the Occupy Wall Street movement described them — have managed to capture a substantial part of the political system for their own benefit. This has happened in all of the capitalist countries in the developed world.

How has that happened, and what are the consequences for Canada? That is what we turn to in the next chapter.

CHAPTER 4

ELITE CONTROL IN A DEMOCRATIC SYSTEM

Whenever you criticize the elite you are setting yourself up to be attacked in return. The basic line is, "You're not successful yourself and so you attack those who have made it." That is not the point. It is not individuals that you are attacking; it is a social and political system that gives the elite rewards that are much greater than others'. It is a question of equality and fairness.

The fact is that many of the corporate elite are very fine people. Some donate generously to their favourite causes. Many in the top positions are well educated and engaged in the social and political life of their communities. They sincerely want the best for the country and their fellow citizens.

But the quality of their character is not the issue. The problems are rooted in the way we practise democracy and capitalism. We value individualism highly, and that has led, in no small part, to entrepreneurism and judging individuals by their accomplishments, particularly the job they hold. But individualism leads to another, more questionable principle: self-interest.

Adam Smith expressed it in this way: "It is not from the benevolence of the butcher, the brewer, or the baker that we expect our dinner, but from their regard for their own interest."[1] In other words, individuals and companies are motivated by self-interest, and that is good because it drives the whole economic system. But this ideology leads to the belief that only the individual's self-interests are considered, not the interests of others or society as a whole.

Self-interest is built into our laws governing for-profit corporations and put directly into the bylaws of many companies. The aim of the corporation, its board of directors, and management is to maximize profits within the laws of the country. Self-interest is a fundamental principle of capitalism. It is what justifies companies seeking corporate welfare. It has been used to justify questionable practices like companies despoiling the environment, unethical accounting practices, and tax breaks that benefit corporations and the wealthy. As we will see, corporations even use self-interest as the reason why they work to gain political influence with government.

*   *   *

LOUDER VOICES

No one familiar with the practice of politics in this country would claim that all citizens have equal influence with our governments. Medical doctors have an important voice over the running of our Medicare system. Farmers have influence over agriculture policies. Lawyers are listened to when the administration of justice is discussed. There are always louder voices on political issues and the loudest are those who have self-interest in the issues.

That is how it should be, but there are some issues that affect us all. Going to war is one. Everyone sacrifices when war is declared, particularly the young people who are drawn into the military. Economic priorities and trade agreements are another set of issues that affect us all.

Corporate leaders have much louder voices than the rest of us on economic issues. It is not difficult to understand why. The state of the economy, particularly the level of unemployment, is very important for the country. The corporate elite is thought to have special insight into the economy because they make investment decisions and lay off and hire people. And yet, why do corporate leaders have such disproportionate influence on these issues? We all are influenced by what happens to the economy.

It can be argued that corporate leaders are the least likely to have informed, objective opinions about economic issues. They are motivated by their self-interest in these questions and the interests of the companies they run. In fact, it is likely that their opinions have been shaped by those interests. That is reason enough to discount their opinions.

And what advice can the corporate elite offer that is so special? Economic issues are influenced by a great number of factors. The dramatic drop in the price of oil in 2015 was totally unexpected by oil analysts. The leaders of oil companies continue to lobby for pipelines, but it may be that, with the drop in demand, the pipelines are unnecessary. In the 1930s the advice of business was that governments should continue to balance budgets. Today we know that was exactly the wrong thing to do. It prolonged the Depression because it shrank the economy.

Despite all of this, the opinions of corporate leaders are valued. But there is another reason why the elite continues to have influence with governments: campaign funding.

* * *

CAMPAIGN FUNDING

Corruption and influence peddling around the funding of election campaigns are as old as Canada itself. The Pacific Scandal, the first major scandal in Canadian history, was all about business buying influence with government.

In the general election of 1872, John A. Macdonald, the Conservative prime minister, was in political trouble and needed money to mount a good campaign in Ontario and Quebec. He and other Conservatives went to see Sir Hugh Allan, a wealthy shipping and railway magnate, and asked for money for the campaign. Allan had ambitions to get the contract to build the transcontinental railway to the Pacific that had been promised to British Columbia. He donated $350,000 to the campaign, worth well over $8 million today. The Conservatives won the election but with a reduced majority. Not long afterward, Allan and the syndicate that he led were awarded the railway contract.

Then the trouble started. The Liberal opposition party revealed that Allan had used American money to supply the campaign funds. More importantly, it was learned that an agreement had been made assuring Allan that he would get the contract to build the railway in return for the money. The most sensational revelation was the telegram sent from John A. Macdonald to Allan's lawyer that read: "I must have another ten thousand; will be the last time of calling; do not fail me; answer today."

The controversy spun out of control and a Royal Commission was struck, but the government could not survive. Macdonald and the Conservatives resigned, an election was called, and the Conservatives lost to the Liberals led by Alexander Mackenzie.[2]

From Macdonald's day until recently corporations have been the major funders of both the Conservatives and the Liberals. There is only scanty evidence about the system of campaign donations and the rewards that flowed from it because the parties and the corporations wanted to keep quiet about it. These are rumours that cannot be verified, but they have a ring of truth about them.

When an election was called, Liberal and Conservative operatives known as "bag men" would go up and down Bay Street in Toronto, and to other corporate offices in the country, to collect money. Big corporations like banks, large manufacturers, and insurance companies would give to both of the major parties: 60 percent to the party in power and 40 percent to the opposition.

Developers and construction companies were always anxious to make campaign donations because many rely on government contracts. Developers, in Ontario at least, were generous but they tended to give money to provincial political parties and municipal politicians, not federal parties, because they relied on approvals from municipal governments. Construction companies gave heavily to municipal politicians, particularly in Quebec.

Was the system of campaign donations corrupt? Not if the companies and parties followed the law, but if it was not illegal it was highly questionable. When money changes hands behind closed doors, many suspect that it was given by companies to receive benefits from the politicians. The important issue is not corruption, but why companies were making large donations to the parties. We know the answer to that. They want influence, and they are willing to pay big bucks to get it.

Governments pass laws that affect companies in various ways. Regulations can be very specific, and force changes in the day-to-day operations of corporations. Companies want influence over those laws and regulations, or at least they want their concerns listened to. One of the ways they can gain influence is by making campaign donations.

But there have been recent changes in election laws. In 2002 the then prime minister Jean Chrétien and his Liberal government introduced legislation to ban corporate and union campaign donations to federal political parties. The money was replaced by a system of government funding of parties depending on the number of votes received in the previous election, and a rebate system when individuals make contributions. There was resistance from politicians and even from Chrétien's own party but the bill passed and became law.[3]

This law has significantly changed how federal elections have been financed. All of the parties had to establish a system in which they gained most of their funding from individuals. As it turned out, the Conservatives, under Stephen Harper, had a well-oiled machine and raised more money than other parties from individual supporters. The NDP for years had depended on individual donors and made the transition to the new system easily. The Liberals, on the other hand, suffered from lack of funds in the early years of the new system.

But did it make any difference? The province of Quebec had laws similar to the federal government barring corporate and union donations, but they were often ignored. In 2013 Quebec's chief electoral officer found that $12.8 million was donated illegally by the employees of 532 companies, mainly construction, engineering, law, and accounting firms. Former employees of one corporation flatly admitted that political contributions had illicitly been made in their names. Both the Liberals and Parti Québécois (PQ) were implicated.[4]

The Charbonneau Commission was established to enquire into political fundraising. It found illegal campaign donations and widespread bid rigging for municipal contracts by construction companies. The mayor of Laval was forced to resign; the mayor of Montreal, Gérald Tremblay, resigned as a result of the allegations; and his replacement, Michael Applebaum, resigned after he was charged with fourteen offences.

In Quebec, it appears, the whole system became corrupt because both the politicians and the corporations conspired to break the law. That is what happened 150 years ago in the Pacific Scandal, and it continues to this day. As long as the system is secret, and players on both sides are willing to break the rules, then the law is useless.

* * *

POLITICAL ACCESS FOR SALE

Soon allegations of irregular political fundraising reached Ontario as well. The federal government, Quebec, and Manitoba passed laws to ban corporate and union donations to political parties, but that was not followed by Ontario and the other provinces. The Liberal provincial government in Ontario, under premiers Dalton McGuinty and Kathleen Wynne, continued to accept corporate donations. In fact, the donations scheme became more sophisticated.

In March 2016 Martin Regg Cohn, the Queen's Park reporter for the *Toronto Star*, published a story called "Revealed: the secret price of admission to power." He detailed how the provincial Liberals had hosted a series of fundraising dinners where lobbyists paid big money for access to cabinet ministers. "At their sumptuous Heritage Dinner, 'Victory Tables' are priced at $18,000 for corporate high flyers, and the biggest donors are fêted at a private cocktail reception by a grateful premier."[5]

Cohn went on to write that the senior members of the Liberal Cabinet were given fundraising targets. The minister of finance, Charles Sousa, was expected to bring in $500,000 every year to the party coffers; the minister of health, Eric Hoskins, between $500,000 and $400,000 every year. Other senior ministers were given targets of between $300,000 and $250,000, and junior ministers were expected to bring in additional monies. The Liberal Party had become a finely tuned machine designed to raise corporate money that would be used during elections.

This was a "payment for access" system, as Cohn called it, and the corporate elite lined up to take advantage of it. By day the job of the cabinet ministers was to supervise and regulate companies, professionals, and individuals operating within their jurisdiction on behalf of the public, but at the fundraising dinners they met and socialized with the very same executives of companies that they were regulating.

This was access for sale. These are two examples. Sousa and the energy minister, Bob Chiarelli, met with executives of the Bank of Nova Scotia, the major underwriter of Hydro One. In another private dinner the energy minister and the premier met with energy insiders. The participants paid $6,000 a person to be at the cocktail party with the cabinet ministers. Both cases were clear conflicts of interest.

Although members of the public were unaware of the existence of these fundraisers at the time, political insiders knew what was going on and many did not like it. Former Liberal finance minister Dwight Duncan told Cohn, "One of the reason I quit [politics was] I was so sick of it.… As minister of finance you are in a portfolio where people want to see you and pay for it.… It is the wrong system."

John Gerretsen, the former attorney general, said that he was deeply troubled by the undeniable conflict of interest. "If a major issues comes up and you have been funded by lobbyists on behalf of any kind of industry you're going to be affected by that … it's human nature."

Editorialists joined the chorus of critics. The *Globe and Mail* wrote, "The Ontario Liberal Party has turned ministers into salespeople, giving them hard quotas and telling them to sell one product every lobbyist wants — uncontrolled access to the levers of government." The editorial went on to point out that it was not only the Liberals at Queen's Park who hosted these funds for access dinners and cocktail parties; the Progressive Conservatives and New Democrats did the same.[6]

As the story broke and the public furor increased, other news agencies published stories about the "access for sale" issue. At first Premier Wynne tried to justify the system, claiming that these fundraising dinners and cocktail parties did not influence political decision making in Ontario, but no one was buying that argument. The only reason a corporate leader would go to a political function like this was to try and gain influence. Within days of the first newspaper story by Martin Regg Cohn, the premier announced that legislation would be changed to make corporate and union donations to political parties illegal.[7]

Soon it was learned that it was not just Ontario where the payment for access system existed. Gary Mason, the *Globe and Mail* reporter in British Columbia, revealed that the Liberal provincial government in that province also had established a similar system. At a recent Vancouver dinner, guests had paid $10,000 for the chance to mingle with Premier Christy Clark. A group at another dinner in Kelowna paid $5,000 for access to the premier.[8]

But Premier Clark proved to be made of sterner stuff than Wynne. When challenged on these practices she said that payment for access events were not illegal and she had no intension of banning corporate and union donations to political parties. She did, however, promise to make political donations more transparent, whatever that means.[9]

Then in October 2016 the federal finance minister, Bill Morneau, participated in a fundraiser with Halifax business people who paid $1,500 per ticket. Again there were denials of any wrongdoing.[10]

* * *

INCOME INEQUALITY AND TAX POLICY

Those who think corporate lobbying makes no or little difference should look at income inequality and how tax policy gives advantages to corporations and the wealthy. This is what the Canadian Centre for Policy Alternatives says about tax fairness: "Canada's tax system is no longer acting as an income equalizer. It has become so regressive that the top 10 percent of earners pay a lower share of income in tax than the poorest 10 percent."[11]

In a new study, David Macdonald of CCPA looked at tax loopholes that allowed some Canadians to reduce the amount of income tax that they paid. He found that 59 out of 64 loopholes were regressive because they favoured those with high incomes. These loopholes amounted to an astounding $100.5 billion a year. Macdonald concludes, "If the federal government got rid of all tax expenditures it would roughly double the amount of income tax collected."[12]

Since the 1970s, income inequality in Canada has been getting worse. Most of the new wealth that has been created has gone to the top 10 percent of income earners and the top 1 percent has taken the lion's share of this. Middle and lower incomes have stagnated. The average for the bottom 50 percent of earners in Canada was $14,900 in 2013, while the top 1 percent was $516,000.[13] One researcher says that the bottom 10 percent has seen its incomes shrink by 150 percent. In 2012 debts for the bottom 10 percent outweighed assets by $5,100.[14] Because the tax system is regressive, and the top income earners pay a lower portion of income on taxes, the tax burden in this country has shifted onto the middle class.

The reason the middle class gets hit with taxes is because it is the easiest target. The wealthy are mobile and they can move to low tax jurisdictions like Barbados, Bermuda, or Monaco. Dozens of corporations have already shifted their corporate headquarters to tax havens.[15] The other reason those with middle incomes are paying more taxes is that corporate taxes have been reduced. In 2000 the corporate tax rate was 29.1 percent. Today it is 15 percent. In the United States, by comparison, the federal corporate tax rate is 35 percent for taxable income over $335,000.

Unlike most developed countries, the United States included, Canada has no inheritance tax, and again, that increases inequality in this country. Wealthy families are able to retain their assets from generation to generation and that increases income inequality.

Tax loopholes and tax credits have been purposely built into the Canadian tax code to benefit the wealthy. The group Canadians for Tax Fairness has identified over $10 billion of tax revenue being lost every year as a result of loopholes.[16]

Canada has developed an over reliance on regressive taxes like property taxes, GST/HST, hidden sales taxes, and charges for services. This has happened because of the growing resistance to increasing income taxes, but this has significant impact on the tax system. Middle- and lower-income Canadians pay a higher proportion of their income on these types of regressive taxes. It is the proportion of income paid in taxes that is important. For a tax system to be progressive it must tax those with higher incomes at a higher rate than those with lower incomes. The reliance on regressive taxes is one of the major reasons that top earners pay a lower proportion of their income in tax than the middle class or the poor.

The problems of the Canadian tax system have been growing in recent decades, and the Stephen Harper Conservative government made it worse. The Justin Trudeau Liberal government has begun to change the system. In 2016, its first year in government, it cancelled the Conservative plan for family income splitting and introduced a new income tax rate of 33 percent for those earning over two hundred thousand dollars a year. Both of those moves helped to slow the increasing income inequality, but there will have to be a reform of all tax policies in Canada before we can claim to have a more progressive tax system.

One final note about income inequality: The World Bank, the IMF, and several leading economists, including Nobel Prize–winner Joseph Stiglitz, warn that growing income inequality is a threat to our democratic values of equality and to our economy. What is happening is that the wealthy class is increasing its savings. The wealthy literally have so much money that they cannot spend it all, a situation that is lowering demand and economic growth but increasing unemployment. All of this results in economic stagnation.

The only way this can change is to create more progressive taxation policies. That will lead to greater government spending on badly needed infrastructure and services and will return the developed world to economic growth.

* * *

TAX HAVENS AND TAX AVOIDANCE

As if the unfairness of our tax policy is not enough, tax avoidance schemes and tax havens are being used to shelter money on a massive scale. It is not illegal for Canadians or corporations to own foreign companies. Many have legitimate investments abroad. But owners of offshore companies go to great lengths to hide their identities. They are putting their money in tax havens to avoid paying taxes back home.

Canadians for Tax Fairness has scoured various sources and estimates that assets held offshore by Canadian corporations amounted to $199 billion in 2015. Canada is now losing $80 billion a year to offshoring funds. This is the amount that is reported in corporate balance sheets. In 1987, 10 percent of Canadian direct investments overseas went to tax havens; in 2011 it had risen to 24 percent. These are estimates of offshore funds held legally. No one has an estimate of how much illegal Canadian money is held in tax havens.[17]

The prime tax havens that Canadians use include Barbados ($71 billion), the Cayman Islands ($36 billion), and Switzerland ($11 billion). Pressure has been put on these and other tax havens to reveal the identities of Canadians who have sheltered their money offshore, but there is great reluctance on the part of legal firms, banks, and countries that handle these funds to reveal anything about them. It is only whistle-blowers, like those who outed the Panama Papers, who have revealed something of the scale of tax avoidance that is going on.

This is a worldwide problem. The international group Tax Justice Network estimates that tax avoidance costs governments around the world more than $3.1 trillion (US) annually. Oxfam recently estimated that the wealthiest 1 percent in the world now control more wealth than the remaining 99 percent. They claim $7.6 trillion is in offshore tax havens.[18] "More than $1 in $6 earned in the world is not subject to tax because those earning it have deliberately ensured that their income is hidden from tax authorities." In Greece and Italy, it is estimated that more than one euro in four is hidden in the shadow economy. The Panama Papers revealed that a number of politicians, corporate leaders, organized crime members, sports figures, and others are using offshore accounts to shelter income.[19]

Knowledge about the shadow economy has been growing, but now we have learned that tax haven schemes were promoted and facilitated by the Canadian government. A *Toronto Star* article, "Tax-Haven Deals Had

Ottawa's Blessing," starts by saying that the "seeds of Canadian corporations hiding billions of dollars in offshore tax havens were sown more than 40 years ago after the Canadian government pursued a series of tax treaties with tiny Caribbean and European nations."[20]

At the time these tax treaties were put in place there were politicians, like Bob Rae, who warned that there would be a huge tax loss. Two Canadian auditor generals, Sheila Fraser and L. Denis Desautels, have criticized the system. In 2002 Sheila Fraser said, "Tax rules that reduced tax revenues mean either higher taxes for other taxpayers, or reductions in public expenditures, and no one wants to pay someone else's taxes…. It's time to fix this." But no government or finance minister has fixed it and the problem of tax avoidance has become much worse.

Recently it was learned that in 2010 the Harper Conservative government approved something called Tax Information Exchange Agreements. This was supposed to crack down on tax cheats who offshored money to tax havens, but it didn't work out that way. The government tweaked the Canadian tax code and as a result of those changes corporations earning profits in a partner country were allowed to bring those profits back to Canada tax-free. That change let corporations bring back about $55 billion into the country without paying taxes on it. If it had been taxed it would have yielded $14 billion in revenue.[21]

Politicians clearly have chosen not to fix any of these problems. Corporations and individuals who offshore funds benefit from Canadian infrastructure like roads, water, and electricity. They also benefit from our public education system, Medicare, and the peace and security of our country, and yet they don't pay their fair share of those costs. They costs have been shifted onto the middle class, who cannot avoid paying their taxes. This, more than anything, demonstrates corporate power in this country.

Aditya Chakrabortty, a journalist for the British newspaper the *Guardian*, writes, "The super-rich have effectively exited the economic system the rest of us have to live in…. 30 years of plutocracy have brought us an era of un-representative democracy."[22]

* * *

DEMOCRACY AND ELITES

The details of these corporate handouts, campaign donations, tax concessions, and the sheltering of money offshore illustrate in a stark way how the wealthy elite of this country have reaped the benefits of our democratic system of government. Now that same corporate elite supports free trade deals with low wage countries that threaten the jobs of working people and lower their incomes.

There are solutions: more progressive income tax, with the wealthy paying a higher proportion of their income than others; an inheritance tax; cancelling the loopholes in our system of taxation; and shutting down the tax havens. It is in the interest of the majority of Canadians to legislate these things, and yet nothing is done. Governments ignore these issues and carry on as if they do not matter, and that clearly demonstrates that they have chosen to support the corporate business elite over the people. Is it any wonder that ordinary people are angry and express their frustration by voting for Brexit and Donald Trump?

It has not always been like this. In the past there have been many different attempts to change politics and gain a better deal for groups of people. Some have been remarkably successful. We are going to look at a number of them in the next section of the book.

PART 2

REFORMERS AND THE GRASSROOTS

Representative democracy and corporate capitalism emerged at about the same time in our history. There can be no doubt that they are linked and have supported and helped each other. The fear that the poor and the working class would use their power at the ballot box to take the property of those with wealth never materialized. All of the efforts to restrict the franchise to exclude those who were dangerous or incompetent proved to be needless.

As early as the middle of the nineteenth century in Canada an arrangement emerged between the political and economic elites that goes something like this. Big business brought investments, created wealth and jobs, and produced goods and services that the people wanted. This generated tax revenue, which the government used to provide grants, land, and other monetary benefits to big business. They put in place a regulatory system that facilitated business interests, provided protection through the legal system, and created a favourable tax system that benefited business and wealthy individuals.

The deal excluded small businesses, and that group has become an important source of opposition to this cozy arrangement because they see no advantage for them. Many have become supporters of right-wing political parties that advocate shrinking down government to reduce costs and taxes. Supporters of the NDP also opposed it. They advocated redistributing wealth to the less fortunate through various programs.

There has always been opposition and resistance from other sources. Some have been reformers trying to improve the conditions of the poor and the excluded. Others have been grassroots organizations and movements. There have been failures and setbacks, but in most cases these efforts have met with some success in spite of sustained opposition from business and government.

What follows are accounts of some of these movements.

CHAPTER 5

TOP-DOWN REFORM: PROGRESSIVES AND THE FARM PARTIES

Prior to the First World War, autocratic governments in Eastern Europe tried to hold on to power through repression. They used police, the army, and secret agents to apply brutal methods and reaped the whirlwind of radicalism and revolution. In North America and western Europe, where forms of representative democracy had been established, the struggle for an equal, democratic society was much more open and lawful. It took different forms.

Some attempts at change involved "top-down" reformism, where those with means tried to ameliorate social problems with services and organizations designed to provide help to those in need. Other efforts of political reform involved trying to win power through the electoral process, and once elected, using the power of government to legislate change. Still others involved efforts to create grassroots organizations and movements that could create changes from below.

In Canada, all of these different strategies were used.

$$* \quad * \quad *$$

THE ROOTS OF SOCIAL REFORM

In the fifty years after the end of the American Civil War in 1864 and up to the outbreak of the First World War in 1914, North America went through unprecedented changes. Cities grew at a phenomenal rate due to immigration and to the migration of people from farms and small towns into the city. Education, at least at a primary level, became universal, and enrollment in high school, colleges, and universities soared. An economic boom between 1895 and 1913 brought prosperity to millions of people. All this led to the emergence of an educated middle class that fundamentally changed North America — both the United States and Canada.

Members of this new middle class were almost entirely white and Protestant. When they looked at the way politics was practised, many were horrified. In the United States corruption was widespread. The muckraking journalists showed that the so-called robber barons had amassed incredible wealth at the expense of the poor and the workers who laboured to produce the wealth.

In both Canada and the United States there were no income or inheritance taxes that could begin to equalize wealth. John D. Rockefeller and Standard Oil Company bought politicians and manipulated the stock market. Henry Clay Frick and Andrew Carnegie controlled steel mills and broke unions in strikes that were more like wars than industrial disputes. And the railway promoters and mining conglomerates of the West controlled the governments of states and municipalities. In Canada the collusion between politicians and the wealthy may not have been as complete, but that was only because the population was not as large and the opportunities for plunder not as great.

The large cities in the United States were dominated by political machines in this era. Tammany Hall, in New York City, was the largest and most effective, but there were machines in Chicago, Boston, Philadelphia, St. Louis, and Kansas City. The city machines depended on the boss, who made the decisions, and a cadre of workers who could deliver the vote. The votes came from immigrants and the poor.

It was a type of patronage system. Once the machine controlled the city, the boss then could deliver essential services to supporters, like welfare, jobs, or handouts when people got into trouble. The machine also delivered graft to the machine boss and the cadre of workers. As George Washington Plunkitt, the Tammany boss of the Fifteenth Assembly District in New York, expressed it, "I seen my opportunities and I took 'em."[1]

All this was justified by the glorification of the individual along with an ideology of Social Darwinism appropriated from Darwin's theory of the survival of the fittest. Darwin had argued that species evolved because the fittest had characteristics that helped them to survive, while the unfit became extinct. In the same way, the argument went, the wealthy were the fittest because they were the wealthiest, and therefore, deserved their wealth.

In the eyes of the rising middle class at that time, this whole system of graft and political influence, controlled by those with wealth, was impossibly corrupt, and they were determined to do something about it. In time they came to be called the Progressives.

* * *

THE PROGRESSIVES

The Progressives saw themselves as modernizers. They believed in science and technology and at the same time they were positive about the new industrial society that was sweeping North America. It was an optimistic movement that believed in individualism, not unlike the wealthy. Many felt that if they could just get the right system, a new, more equal, and less corrupt society would emerge in America.

Historians say the Progressive Era stretches from about 1890 to 1920, but its influence goes far beyond this. The urban middle class, where they drew their strongest support, was hardly a majority of North American society. At that time about 40 percent of the people lived on farms, and a large proportion of people living in urban areas worked in factories or in other manual occupations.

The Progressives did not have the support of the Catholics, who had influence with the urban poor and the working class, or of the evangelical churches, which were powerful in rural areas. They were a minority, but they had powerful allies in key political, educational, and social positions like the large, established Protestant churches. This new middle class was energetic and future oriented. Above all, they felt they had progress on their side.

In the United States the Progressives were a political movement that influenced both the Republicans and the Democrats. Three American presidents identified themselves as Progressives: Republicans Theodore Roosevelt (1901–09) and William Howard Taft (1909–13), and Democrat Woodrow Wilson (1913–21). (In 1912 Teddy Roosevelt ran for president on the Progressive ticket and lost. The party collapsed and Progressives went back to the practice of supporting both major parties.)

Reforming local government was a major focus of the movement. They tried to eliminate the power and corruption of the urban political machines. Although education was largely a local responsibility, they worked to expand and improve the quality of the educational system. Teacher training colleges were established, and high schools were built in the cities. Education improved dramatically.

Even post-secondary educational institutions felt the influence of the Progressives. They founded scores of colleges and universities. Many states established state-run universities where students could study by paying modest tuition fees. The Progressives promoted the social sciences of economics, political science, and sociology because they believed that political decisions should be based on facts and science, not prejudice and unfounded opinion. The teaching of medicine was centralized in the universities at this time. Treatment became based on science, not traditional healing methods. Even the practice of law became more academic, replacing the old system where lawyers took on assistants and trained them much like apprentices learning a trade.

Children were a particular concern for the Progressives. Child neglect was common in urban slums, and the lack of good nutrition was widespread. Groups like the Scouting and Guiding organizations were founded at this time as a way to promote healthy living, honesty, and proper moral behaviour. Recreation and sports were promoted. Urban parks were built so people could have recreation and sunshine. It was the Progressives who promoted national parks in Canada and the United States. Some of the Progressives even promoted birth control so the poor could cut high birth rates. This was a radical act because birth control was illegal in most jurisdictions in North America.

The Progressives used their political influence to enact legislation. They were very concerned about the power of monopolies, and at this time the first anti-trust laws were legislated in the United States. New financial regulations were put in place to control the speculation of banks and other financial institutions. Laws on the pasteurization of milk were passed, and sanitary conditions in meat packing plants were introduced thanks to their efforts. It was Progressives that introduced legislation for referendums on important issues. This practice began in the state of Oregon and spread to other states and provinces, particularly in the west.

The women's movement was deeply influenced by the Progressives, and their interest in family and home was a dominant theme in the movement. Virtually all of the suffragettes considered themselves part of the Progressive Movement in both Canada and the United States. One special issue supported by women at the time was the prohibition of alcohol. The demand to make alcohol consumption illegal goes back to the 1840s. The Women's Christian Temperance Union (WCTU) was founded in 1874 and it became one of the leading organizations dedicated to stamping out alcohol.

Many — but not all — of the men who identified as Progressives supported prohibition. It was believed that the urban political machines were organized in saloons, and some saw prohibition as a way to attack the machines. But women saw the banning of alcohol as a way of protecting wives and children from drunken husbands. There was a great deal of heavy drinking at this time. Alcohol was cheap and plentiful.

In the years leading up the First World War women were becoming much more politically active. They were demanding the vote and reform on a large number of issues, including the outright banning of the manufacturing, distribution, sale, and consumption of alcohol. They were a powerful organized constituency that no politician could ignore. It is no accident that 1920 was the year that women were granted the vote in the United States, and in the same year the Volstead Act, that banned manufacturing, distribution, and sale of alcohol, was enacted. In Canada women got the vote during the First World War, and within months prohibition was legislated as part of the war effort.

Prohibition proved to be a colossal failure, one that reflected badly on the Progressive Movement. It spawned an unprecedented level of criminal activity with the illegal trade that arose to get around it. By 1925 prohibition was repealed in most provinces, and the Volstead Act was finally rescinded in 1933. It is tempting to say that prohibition was the reason for the decline of the Progressive Movement, and it did play a role, but by 1920 the demands for social reform were fading. The Bolshevik Revolution in Russia led to concerns about the rise of communism, and that in turn led to the "Red Scare." In the 1920s times were good, the stock market was booming, and the middle class developed other interests. Business gained new prestige and social reform efforts began to fade.

If there was a moment in the history of the United States when the Progressive movement could be said to have died, it would be when Franklin

Delano Roosevelt announced the New Deal in 1933. What Progressives remained in Congress voted against the New Deal programs because they felt it was too reliant on government and not enough on the individual.

And yet the movement was hardly a failure. In one sense all of us are Progressives today because their core ideas are deeply embedded in our society and the social reform movement that continues. That is particularly true in Canada.

* * *

THE CANADIAN PROGRESSIVES

Social reform in Canada was deeply influenced by the Progressive movement of the United States. In the fifty years before the First World War, Canada — like the United States — went through rapid social changes. The middle class grew prosperous and the established Protestant churches were very influential. Like in the United States, there was concern in Canada for the poor and the new immigrants who were arriving by the thousands.

Education was a special concern in Canada. Child labour, inadequate housing, urban slums, the need for pure food, the integration of immigrants, all of these issues were important to the middle-class progressives. The parallel with women's issues in both countries is also striking. Women in Canada and the United States got the vote within two years of each other; prohibition was legislated in both countries within months of women getting the vote in both countries.

But after the war Canadian politics and the social reform movement took a very different direction from the United States. There were many reasons for this. Canadian cities were growing rapidly, but they were never as large or unmanageable as their U.S. counterparts. Montreal, the largest city in the country in 1921, had a population of 618,506; Toronto, 521,893; Winnipeg, 179,087; and Vancouver, 162,229.[2] New York, by contrast, had a population of 5.5 million; Chicago, 2.7 million; and Philadelphia, 1.8 million.[3]

Our British links also brought us a great number of British immigrants both before and after the war, who influenced the political and social life of this country. Many of them brought the tradition of Fabian socialism with them, which they had learned through British trade unions and the Labour Party. They demanded political reforms that came from working-class organizations, particularly the unions, and advocated a strategy that called for taking over government by democratic means to achieve those demands. It was very different than the middle-class Progressive movement from south of the border, and it was an influence on the political life of this country.

The impact of the First World War on Canada was much greater than on the United States. Canadians had fought in the trenches for the four-year duration of the war, while the Americans fought for only a year and a half. Canadians suffered a much higher rate of casualties. The United States came out of the war as a leading world power, affluent, confident, and with a booming economy. Canadians were proud of the sacrifices that were made, but there was also anger and resentment directed toward our political leaders, who led the country into this tragedy only because of our links to the British Empire. There was a sharp recession right after the war, and during the 1920s there was economic instability. All this was just a precursor to the economic disaster of the Great Depression.

* * *

THE FARM PARTIES

The social reforms promoted by the Progressives focused primarily on cities in Canada and the United States, but rural areas had their own problems. In Canada a special issue for farmers was high tariffs.

John A. Macdonald, and his Conservatives, had legislated the National Policy of high tariffs in 1879. Farmers opposed tariffs because it meant high prices for things like farm machinery and other manufactured products. The United States also had high tariffs and that restricted Canadian goods. The Liberals promised free trade, but when they gained power in 1896 under the leadership of Wilfrid Laurier, there was little they could do to keep that promise because Americans refused to reduce their tariffs.

In 1911 Laurier's government negotiated an agreement with the Americans for the free trade of agricultural goods. This became very controversial with the Conservative opposition, who claimed it would lead to an American takeover of the country. To resolve the issue, Laurier called an election and lost to the Conservatives. Farmers were deeply disappointed and many were determined to do something about it.

Farmers had always worked co-operatively, both at busy times of year, such as planting and harvest, and to solve common problems. Co-operatives had become an important feature of Ontario rural life, and with the settlement of the West, co-ops became a central organization on the Prairies.

Even before the Great War, farmers were becoming increasingly political. In 1914 the United Farmers of Ontario (UFO) began to organize as a political party. They advocated farmer's issues like the nationalization of the railways, progressive taxation, and legislation to protect co-operatives. The UFO also were strong supporters of prohibition. The party grew rapidly so that by 1919 it had more than fifty thousand members.

Immediately after the First World War political agitation was at a fever pitch all across Canada. Unemployment was high. Returning soldiers came home to find there were no jobs. Immigrants crowded into cities seeking relief. There was talk of the Bolshevik Revolution among workers, and a rising fear of radicals among the members of the Conservative government in Ottawa. Then, in May of 1919, the Winnipeg General Strike broke out, which lasted for three months before it was put down by the federal government and the Royal Northwest Mounted Police.

In the 1919 Ontario provincial election the UFO mounted sixty-four candidates in rural ridings. Their platform was reformist: the end of political patronage, better education in rural areas, cheap hydro, and protecting forests. The unions were also organizing politically into the newly formed Independent Labour Party (ILP), which contested twenty urban ridings. To the shock of everyone on Election Day, the farmers won forty-five seats and were the largest party in the legislature. They entered into a coalition with the ten elected ILP members and became the government under the leadership of Premier Ernest Drury.

The Ontario Farm–Labour (FL) government brought in a number of reforms. They created a provincial welfare department, provided support for widows and orphans, expanded Ontario Hydro, and established a Province of Ontario Savings Office, among other things. Prohibition enforcement proved to be difficult and controversial. There was little support for a ban on alcohol in cities. Workers were strongly opposed, but in rural areas prohibition still had the fervor of a religious crusade. This split the FL coalition. Rum-running in border crossings like Windsor and along the Niagara River grew rapidly.

There were mounting political problems for the coalition while at the same time the Conservative Party reorganized under the leadership of Howard Ferguson, a lawyer from eastern Ontario. In the 1923 election the Drury government lost to the Conservatives, who promised to legalize alcohol but with government control. (This is the origin of the LCBO and other provincial liquor control boards.)

The United Farmers of Alberta (UFA) was more successful electorally than its counterpart in Ontario. The UFA had been founded as a lobby group in 1913, but the success of other Farm Parties convinced it to run as a political party in the 1921 provincial election. It won a majority government and held power until 1935.

The UFA had an active legislative agenda. They improved medical care in the province, broadened the rights of labour, and created the Alberta Wheat Pool. The provincial caucus made itself unpopular with many of their rural members by ending prohibition, but one improvement the UFA is remembered for is that under its leadership the province was able to gain control of natural resources from the federal government. (That allowed Alberta to control the oil industry and gain tax revenue from the boom in recent years.)

Finally, the drop in the price of wheat ended the fifteen years of the Farm government during the Depression in 1935. It was replaced by the Social Credit Party, led by William Aberhart, who appealed to the electorate with a promise of financial credit at no interest and with evangelical Protestantism. Today the United Farmers of Alberta continue to exist as a co-operative. They own and operate a successful chain of co-op farm and ranch supply stores and co-op gas stations.

Federally the farm parties, organized on a provincial level, were loosely allied to the Progressive Party, a federal political party that took its name from the Progressive movement. Thomas Crerar, a minister of agriculture in the Unionist government of Robert Borden during the First World War, resigned his cabinet position to protest the government's farm policies. Along with others, he formed the Progressive Party in 1920. In the 1921 federal election the Progressives won fifty-eight of the seats in the Parliament, most from Ontario and Alberta.

From the beginning the Progressives had leadership problems. Crerar was named the leader of the parliamentary caucus, not the party. He resigned in 1921 and the party went into a long, slow decline through the 1920s and 1930s. In time the Alberta members dropped the name Progressive and called themselves representatives of the United Farmers of Alberta. The Ginger Group was the name taken on by a small group of radicals who sat in the opposition benches as members of either the Progressives or Labour. With the Depression of the 1930s the Progressives splintered. Many joined the Liberals. The Ginger Group became founding members of the Co-operative Commonwealth Federation (CCF) in 1932.

In 1921 the United Farmers of Manitoba entered provincial politics and in 1922 they were elected as a majority government. John Bracken became their leader and the party adopted the name the Progressive Party of Manitoba. That party stayed in power, with Bracken as its leader, until the 1940s. In 1942 Bracken left provincial politics with a small number of followers to become the leader of the federal Conservatives. That was when the name of that party was changed to the Progressive Conservative Party of Canada.

It was the economic crisis of the Depression of the 1930s that changed the political reform movement in Canada. Many joined the two established parties, the Liberals and the Conservatives. Those on the democratic left joined the CCF. In 1933 they adopted the Regina Manifesto, a socialist document that expressed the objectives of the party for many years. It called for the public ownership of key industries, pensions, health care, unemployment insurance, children's allowances, and workers compensation. The conclusion reads, "No CCF Government will rest content until it has eradicated capitalism."[4]

Since the founding convention, the party has had many successes and disappointments. In 1961 the CCF made an alliance with the labour movement and adopted the name the New Democratic Party (NDP). Today it is a social democratic party like the Social Democrats of Scandinavia. Federally the party has never formed a government. Its greatest success has been at the provincial level.

* * *

PROGRESSIVES AND PARTIES

Some argue that the struggles for social reform over the last 150 years have made no difference. That is nonsense. Reformers have improved the lives of countless people, though it has not led to fundamental change.

The Progressives were middle-class reformers who never challenged the elites and that explains why they were accepted so readily. The Farm Parties were reformers in a different way. They came from modest roots. They went into politics because the farm economy was in crisis, but like the Progressives, their policies never challenged elite control. Both movements shared a top-down strategy that imposed reform from above.

But there is another strategy: bottom-up change from below. These are grassroots groups who challenge the cozy arrangement of the political and business elites that see the major role of government as support for corporate interests.

Next, we are going to look at the grassroots organizations that fought the longest and have gained the most in their challenge of elites: the trade union movement.

CHAPTER 6

TRADE UNIONS

Unions are practical, grassroots organizations of workers that protect the rights of their members in the workplace, and strive to enhance wages, pensions, and other benefits.

The strategy of unions has been to work co-operatively with employers, but to use the power of a strike when necessary to gain their objectives. Through their history, they have remained stubbornly independent and ready to use confrontation. In that sense they have never been reformist.

The rise of unions has been well documented, but one important element has often been forgotten. Prior to the Second World War there was a deep-seated prejudice against manual workers in Canada and other countries. For decades those without property were denied the vote. In the workplace, they faced rigid discipline. They even found it difficult to get credit that could help to improve their lives. The divide between the working class, the middle class, and the elite was enormous.

Because of this the struggle for unions was always much more than an effort to improve the living standards of workers and their families. It was a struggle for respect, and in a fundamental way, a struggle for equality and democracy.

* * *

FROM INDEPENDENT PRODUCERS TO INDUSTRIAL WORKERS

Prior to 1800, most people who lived in the territory that we now call Canada were independent producers who worked for themselves in the commodity trades. Fishermen on the Atlantic coast caught and cured codfish. The merchants marketed the catch and kept most of the profits. In the fur trade it was native people who trapped and cured the furs while the Hudson's Bay Company dominated the trade because they marketed the furs.

For much of the nineteenth century the timber trade was the most important Canadian export. Thousands of men spent their winters in the bush in New Brunswick, Quebec, and the Upper Ottawa River Valley and drove the logs downriver in the spring drive. The timber was exported mainly to Britain out of ports like Miramichi and Quebec City. As settlement spread and farms produced surpluses, the export of grain became important. Gradually a more settled life developed, and with the growth of towns and cities, a different type of economy emerged.

Independent craftsmen set up workshops: blacksmiths, coopers, tailors, shoemakers, and many other trades. They would take on apprentices (some younger than ten years old) who became journeymen as they grew older and learned their trade, eventually becoming craftsmen in their own right. It was not long before larger shops developed where tradesmen worked for others and earned wages. When that happened they were no longer independent producers; they were employees who worked at the direction of their employers. An independent producer set his own hours and controlled the shop where he worked, but when he became an employee he lost that power. Even his way of life was now controlled by his employer.

The work in those early shops was grim. Ten- to twelve-hour days, six days a week was standard in the early part of the nineteenth century. It could be dangerous and injuries were common. Apprentices were indentured and lived with their masters, who had the responsibility of parents. Often young boys were beaten and brutally treated. They could be fined, their wages withheld, and if they ran away, they would be picked up by the police and imprisoned. (Not until 1891 in Ontario were children required to go to school until they were fourteen years of age.)[1]

As the factory system became widespread after 1870, discipline became more rigid. There were beatings for minor infractions, fines, and some employers had a "black hole" in the basement of their factories where unruly or rebellious workers were locked up for short periods. Employers kept blacklists of troublemakers they refused to hire. In the coal mining districts of Cape Breton and Nova Scotia, companies often provided housing and a company store for the miners and their families. Often the miners were paid in script that they could only cash at the company store. The conditions of the houses were bad, and the food overpriced. That gave employers more control over their workers and more opportunity to make profits.

Unemployment was a constant concern of workers. Pay was so low, particularly for the unskilled, that they had few savings. With a downturn in the economy they would be laid off and soon face poverty. There are examples of food riots in Montreal when desperate workers attacked bread wagons to get something to eat. The old and the infirm, who had no family, soon were forced into the municipally run House of Industry, the nineteenth-century term for the Poor House.

Perhaps the worst examples of terrible working conditions in Canada were in the building and improvement of the canals on the St. Lawrence River and the Great Lakes during the 1840s. These were the first large-scale projects in the county that employed thousands of workers. Many were impoverished, recently arrived, unskilled Irish labourers, but there were some French Canadian workers and others. The big projects were the Lachine and Beauharnois Canals near Montreal and the Welland Canal in the Niagara Peninsula. The work was hard physical labour for long hours at low pay. The men lived in rough camps they constructed themselves along the canal. Most were single men but a number had wives and young children living with them in the shantytowns. Cholera in the camps was common. There was unemployment in the winter, and on occasion contractors disappeared before paying their workers.

On a number of occasions, the workers rebelled. Strikes broke out with regularity. In 1842 the Welland Canal workers marched brazenly through nearby towns demanding "bread or work." They set fires and dumped equipment into the river. The local townspeople feared violence and insurrection. There was concern that the workers were storing firearms, waiting for the chance to openly revolt. But gradually the volatile situation calmed. It was only resolved when the projects were completed and the workers dispersed.

But despite the danger and hardships, workers throughout this period struggled to increase wages and improve the conditions of work in the shops and factories. Some did that individually but most soon learned that one worker was defenceless. If they worked together, and remained united in their demands, they would have a chance to gain improvements. Unions were the way to do that.

In his book *Working Class Experience*, Bryan D. Palmer lists scores of Canadian unions going back as early as 1798 and many more as the nineteenth century progressed. These were unions of craftsmen. They include carpenters, mechanics, bricklayers, tailors, shoemakers, and others.[2] Skilled workers had the most power because they had the knowledge and skill needed by the employer. Strikes were common but most were short, often lasting only a day or two, designed to force the employer to negotiate on the workers' grievances. Gradually over the nineteenth century the working conditions and rates of pay improved. It is the unions who deserve the credit for those improvements.

There was a strong social element to the craft unions in the latter half of the nineteenth century. The members were proud of their skill, and they wanted to demonstrate their value to the community. Many unions had rituals and secret signs to show they were member of the brotherhood. Elaborate dinners with formal speeches by dignitaries were common. Often union members paraded in ceremonial processions on holidays and special occasions, displaying their banners and flags. Some unions had funds to support members who became sick or injured. Most collected money so a member could have a dignified funeral, an important ritual in nineteenth-century life.

By the 1870s the Nine Hour League emerged, an organization that was quite different than the craft unions. Before its emergence most union action focused on a particular shop or factory. The Nine Hour League was a collective effort of many different unions in central Canada from Montreal, Toronto, Hamilton, and southwestern Ontario to reduce the hours of work to nine a day. Meetings were held, a giant procession of workers was staged in Hamilton with a formal dance that evening, and a strike was called. Ultimately the strike failed and the ten-hour workdays continued, but this was the first time that a broad collective action had been staged by many workers in a number of different unions and crafts.

In the process of fighting for the nine-hour day the typographical workers of the *Globe* newspaper in Toronto went out on strike. The publisher, George Brown, a fervent believer in the ideology of liberalism, free enterprise, and competition, saw the strike as an illegal interruption of trade. That led to the arrest of twenty-four of the *Globe*'s printers. The courts ruled that strikes and unions were illegal. John A. Macdonald, the Conservative prime minister, saw this as an opportunity to attack his Liberal opponent, and he passed the Trades Union Bill. The legislation said that unions were legal. It was weak and provided no protection for the unionists, but it still gained the support of trade union members for the Conservative Party for a decade or more.

* * *

KNIGHTS AND CRAFTSMEN

The Noble and Holy Order of the Knights of Labor was founded in Philadelphia in 1869, and soon gained a huge following by workers across North America. It was quite a different organization than the craft unions that dominated the union movement.

The Knights were highly idealistic. They displayed a pride in working-class culture and labour solidarity. They attempted to unite all workers to oppose exploitation and oppression and believed in no distinctions between people of different colour, ethnicity, belief, or gender. Unlike the craft unions, the Knights would accept as members all workers, skilled and unskilled alike. This was a secret society with oaths and rituals, like many other mutual societies at that time. As Palmer writes, it "was to combine aspects of a religious brotherhood, a political reform society, a fraternal order, and a pure and simple unionism."[3]

Unlike the craft unions, women were welcome in the Knights and many became active members, leading various causes. By the 1880s women were being hired in increasing numbers, particularly in industries like textiles. By 1886 there were more than two hundred local assemblies of women in North America, but most women members were integrated into the local assemblies and were accepted as equals with the men.

The high point of the movement was in the early and mid-1880s, a time of industrial expansion in Canada. Cities grew dramatically and the transcontinental railway was completed, increasing the country's economic potential enormously. The number of employees in manufacturing rose from 87,000 to 166,000 between 1871 and 1891.[4] With the growth of factories came the deskilling of work, and that increased the number of unskilled, rather than skilled, workers.

In this favourable economic climate, the Knights grew rapidly in the industrial heartland of Canada, southern Ontario and the Montreal region. It also spread through the Maritime provinces and as far west as the coal miners in British Columbia. In Quebec there was fierce opposition by the Church, and that kept the numbers down, but many French-speaking workers joined the movement regardless of the views of the Catholic clergy.

The 1880s saw the growth of other workers' organizations. In Cape Breton Island the Provincial Workman's Association organized among the coal miners. On the west coast, the coal miners of Vancouver Island were engaged in a long, bitter struggle against Robert Dunsmuir, the anti-union owner of the mines. They organized secret union societies for fear of punishment. One of their demands was the elimination of Chinese workers from the mines because they had been used by the company as scabs to break strikes and worked for lower wages.

The Knights played a role in the encouragement of political participation. Some members ran for political office at a municipal level, and labour candidates ran for office at the provincial and federal levels, usually in association with the established Liberal and Conservative Parties. Prime Minister Macdonald realized the growing support of labour and made a number of concessions to gain their support. The most important for us, decades later, was his establishment of the Royal Commission on the Relations of Labor and Capital in Canada. This commission toured Canada taking testimony from a great number of witnesses from all classes. It is a rich source of information about working-class life in that era.

But despite all of the success of the Knights, their impact on the Canadian trade union movement and the country was short. Their focus was on broader social and political issues that were national in scope. The interest of unionists, on the other hand, tends to be local problems: working conditions in a factory, or negotiations with employers on wages. The workers wanted direct action with employers, practical reforms, not fine statements on government policy, and it was the old craft unions that were able to deliver that type of practical, pragmatic, "bread and butter" unionism.

The Knights were particularly criticized for their reluctance to call strikes. They encouraged negotiation with employers and arbitration on occasion.

They were criticized for losing the opportunity to strike when it was favourable for workers. This lack of militancy may or may not have been true, but it was perceived to be the case. Workers were becoming more militant and demanded action. By the late 1880s and 1990s the Knights were in decline.

In 1902 at the Trades and Labour Congress of Canada in Berlin (now Kitchener), all those who opposed international unions were banned from the Congress. That drove the Knights from organized labour. Craft unions, the so-called aristocrats of labour, were in firm control of the established trade union movement in both Canada and the United States, but union militancy was rising.

* * *

MONOPOLY CAPITALISM, RADICALS, AND CONFRONTATION

Canada experienced boom times from 1896 to 1913 and that changed everything. This era saw the emergence of monopoly capitalism with the concentration of production into massive industrial complexes. Reducing the costs of production became the essential ingredient of success. Engineers designed and implemented complex production techniques, and mechanization spread. There were scores of corporate mergers. Companies were listed on the stock market, and huge fortunes were made. Banks, gas and oil, steel, textiles, pulp and paper: industry after industry was affected by the changes and the companies that could not adapt soon failed.

This led to major changes in working conditions and the nature of work. Unskilled work increased, and the craftsman's control over the work process was eroded, or eliminated altogether as the skill was designed into the machine. In many cases workers became machine tenders and worked at the pace of the machine. Henry Ford and his engineers designed the assembly line, where workers had to perform the same task, over and over again, as the automobile passed their workstations. The assembly line was adopted rapidly by other companies and other industries. Fredrick Taylor and his followers brought the concept of "scientific management" to the workplace. Workers' movements were timed to find the best, most efficient way to do the job. In industry after industry the speed and pace of the work increased.

Industrial workers were controlled at every moment of the workday. They punched time clocks at the beginning of the work shift and at the end. A worker could not take a bathroom break without permission of the foreman. Those who could not keep up the pace of the work were soon fired. Autocratic foremen ruled the workplace and were often hated and resented by the workers. In many factories makeup gangs of unskilled workers were hired by the day. The foremen in Hamilton steel mills picked men who were either his favourites or those who slipped him a little money so they could get the job.

The growth of unskilled work in Canada was a boom for some. There was still migration of the unemployed from the country into the industrial cities, but most of the new workers came from immigration. There were 2,206,342 new arrivals in Canada from 1903 to 1912; this in a country where the 1911 census recorded only 7,206,643 people. The bulk of the immigrants were from Britain but large numbers hailed from southern and eastern Europe as well. Some settled on homesteads on the Prairies but most of the men became unskilled labourers in factories, mines, railways, and large construction projects. Many of the women worked in the needle trades and textile mills. The pay was poor for the unskilled new Canadians, but the justification was that this work was better than the poverty conditions of their home countries.

The trade union movement was unprepared for these changes. The craft unions refused to organize unskilled workers, but that was where there was growth in the labour market. Strikes broke out with increasing frequency around wages and wage cuts but also issues such as complaints of arbitrary foremen, the pace of work, and attempts to stop the introduction of new technology that eliminated jobs.[5]

There was increased political activity. The Independent Labour Party (ILP) was formed in Ontario and other cities across the country, modelled on the British Labour Party. Marxist Parties were formed and their members became active in local unions. Allan Studholme was elected to the Ontario legislature in a working-class Hamilton riding in 1906 for the ILP. He won a number of elections and served until his death in 1919. Socialists were active across the industrial belt from Montreal to London, Ontario.

In the west of the United States, the Industrial Workers of the World, the IWW, often known as the Wobblies, was formed in 1905. It had a major impact on workers in western Canada and the mines of northern Ontario. The Wobblies had an ideology of direct action. Every member was an independent organizer. They led numerous strikes. Groups of Wobblies would descend on towns when there were strikes, or where free speech was denied. There would be mass protests and local authorities would react with scores of arrests. As time went on there was increased resistance from companies, and repression from governments and police. Many of the Wobblies' leading organizers were charged and convicted of serious crimes.

This turmoil cooled in 1913 with a sharp downturn in the economy. The next summer began the First World War, which lasted for four years and also led to a decrease in militancy. Canadians were committed to the war effort. More than 600,000 Canadians served in the military; 59,544 were killed and more than 170,000 wounded, many with injuries that left them crippled for life. This out of a population of only eight million people.

On the home front during the war, women entered the labour force, working in heavy industry and armament factories. There was virtually no unemployment. Inflation rose faster than wages and that led to the erosion of the standard of living. There were accusations of wartime profiteering by companies that benefited the wealthy.

After the war the economy went into a deep recession. When the soldiers returned home in 1919, they faced unemployment. Radicalism again was on the rise. There was talk of the Bolshevik Revolution in Russia. Strikes broke out. In March 1919 a meeting of labour activists in Calgary founded a group they called the One Big Union, an organization committed to socialism, industrial unionism, and organizing unskilled workers. Then in May 1919 the Winnipeg General Strike broke out.[6]

The strike began with the building trades workers demanding an increase in wages. The metal trades then struck, asking for a forty-four-hour working week and higher wages. The opposition from employers stiffened. On May 13 the Winnipeg Trades Council supported a general strike and two days later over 22,000 workers were on the street. The strike was to grow to involve between 30,000 and 35,000 unionized and un-unionized workers, skilled and unskilled.

The Winnipeg General Strike is the key labour event of this period. It was fought in a dramatic way with mounting confrontations that were reported daily on the front pages of newspapers across Canada and the world. Initially it was a strike for better wages and working conditions, but it soon became a broader confrontation between labour and capital with the government allied with business interests. For some it was a strike demanding political action to deal with worker grievances, for others it was an expression of the underlying anger of workers and their supporters, but for most it remained a strike to improve conditions at work and living standards.

The response to the strike from Winnipeg employers was to form a Citizens' Committee of One Thousand to suppress the strike. They made accusations that strikers were making a "deliberate, criminal and fantastic attempt to make a revolution." Leaders were accused of being Bolsheviks whose actions were "seditious and treasonous."[7]

The responses by strike leaders were equally emotional and heated, but their comments were drowned out in the news coverage. Events escalated. Two hundred and fifty policemen were dismissed because they were said to be sympathetic to the strikers. Postmen were fired from their jobs. The Royal Northwest Mounted Police raided union halls. Leaders were thrown in jail.

In the end the Mounted Police, on horseback, charged a crowd of peaceful strikers, leaving thirty injured and one dead. On June 26, six weeks after the start of the strike, the Central Strike Committee declared the strike over. They could not continue in the face of sustained state repression.

* * *

DECLINE AND ASCENDENCY

The defeat in Winnipeg led to the decline of unions across Canada in the 1920s. The craft unions continued to be the largest organizations, but union membership shrank along with the number of strikes. The strikes that did happen often resulted in defeat. This was the era of the open shop and many in the rank and file saw no point in joining because unions could deliver very little without meaningful solidarity.

Meanwhile there was a new wave of corporate mergers and concentration of economic power in the large corporations. Tariffs were high in both Canada and the United States and more American branch plants located in this country to get under the tariff barrier. This contributed to the Americanization of our economy and culture. Fortunes were made by the speculators as the stock market drifted upwards while the standards of living of working people stagnated or decreased.

Radicalism on the plant floor declined, but in 1921 a group met in a barn near Guelph, Ontario, and founded the Canadian Communist Party. They were dedicated political activists, never large in number, but they had a major impact on the trade union movement for the next twenty-five years. A problem the Canadian communists faced was that the party followed the Moscow line set by the Communist International in Moscow. That forced them to try and adapt policies made in the Soviet Union to Canadian conditions, a difficult challenge, but they were a small, united group with strong party discipline and clear policies.

In the 1920s the Communists advocated the formation of industrial unions, a much different organizational model than the craft unions that continued to dominate the movement. The craft unions organized along craft lines. The mechanics were in one union, the boilermakers in another, the carpenters in another, and so on. In a large factory there could be a number of different unions, and the unskilled had no union at all. That created organizational problems and complicated negotiations. When one craft union went on strike they had to depend on the solidarity of the others to honour their picket lines.

The organizing model of industrial unions was that all workers at a workplace, skilled or unskilled, were in the same union. The United Mine Workers was organized along industrial lines. All the miners and the skilled workers working in the mine belonged to the same union. This made the union stronger and more united during negotiations, particularly in times of strikes. But the craft unions opposed this organizational structure because they felt it weakened their negotiating position.

After the 1929 stock market crash, economic conditions soon became a crisis in Canada. For ten years unemployment was high and the hardships for working people were severe. The winter of 1932–33 was the depth of the Depression when 32 percent of wage earners were unemployed, almost 20 percent of the entire workforce of the country. Many were forced onto relief, where rigid rules dictated that they were not allowed to drink alcohol or spend money on gasoline for their cars.

Strikes almost disappeared in the Depression, and unions barely survived in a very hostile environment. Political agitation increased and with it police harassment of the unemployed. Young men who were out of work travelled the country, jumping on freight trains and "riding the rods." Hobo villages outside cities and towns became common. On the Prairies the economic crisis was worsened by drought, plagues of grasshoppers, and low prices for grain. Many lost their farms.

Young, itinerant men were not allowed welfare in most municipalities during the 1930s. The Conservative government of R.B. Bennett (1930–35), concerned about the mounting political agitation and threats of the young unemployed, established work camps where men would get their room and board and were given make-work jobs, or put to work in national parks. They were paid twenty cents a day. The camps were run by the Canadian military with military discipline. This only led to hostility and rebellion.

In British Columbia in April 1935, fifteen hundred unemployed men in work camps struck and descended on Vancouver. For six weeks they marched the streets, held tag days to raise money for food, had meetings to talk politics, and protested. When one of the unemployed suggested they go to Ottawa to take their demands to R.B. Bennett, the On to Ottawa Trek was born.

Young, unemployed men boarded freight trains heading for Ottawa. Bennett vowed the trekkers would go no further east than Regina. The prime minister did meet with a delegation of the unemployed, but no concessions were made. The march ended on July 1 in Regina when the RCMP attacked the men in the fairgrounds where they were camped. A riot broke out. Pitched battles were fought between the police and the trekkers. Several of the unemployed were injured and one policeman was killed.

The Workers Unity League (WUL) had played a role in the strike and the On to Ottawa Trek. It was a communist-led organization and that gave the prime minister the opportunity to claim that this was an effort to create a revolution. The WUL was very active in the 1930s, leading demonstrations and political groups, but their most important effort was to create new industrial unions under communist leadership.

They were having success among auto workers and steel workers in Ontario, loggers and longshoremen in British Columbia, and in many other plants and worksites across the country. Workers were tired of the insecurity, unemployment, low pay, and abuse handed out by authoritarian foremen. It could cost workers their jobs if they were found to be organizing a union, so most of this organization was done clandestinely; meetings were held in secret away from company property, and discussions about the advantages of union organization were kept quiet.

In the United States the Depression had created similar conditions for working people as in Canada. The debate in the American Federation of Labor (AFL) between the craft unions and those who favoured industrial organization was very intense. It came to a head in the AFL convention in 1935 when John L. Lewis, the head of the United Mine Workers, got into an argument with William Hutcheson, the president of the Carpenters Union. It ended when Lewis punched the carpenter. That punch became a symbolic act that led to the formation of the Congress of Industrial Organizations (CIO) and ultimately a split between the AFL and the CIO.

As this was going on in the United States, President Roosevelt was implementing the New Deal. In May 1935 the Wagner Act, which gave workers the right to join a union of their choice and to bargain collectively with their employers, was passed. Finally, unions and union activities were protected by law. It has proven to be the most important legislation promoting industrial relations in U.S. history.

The CIO quickly went from success to success in the United States. First, the electrical plants were organized by the United Electrical Workers. Second, a sit-down strike was instigated by workers at the General Motors automobile assembly plant in Flint, Michigan, in December 1936. This was a risky strategy because it occupied company property and was illegal. It reflects the level of militancy of the rank and file. By mid-February GM had capitulated, the United Automobile Workers were recognized, and the company agreed to a 5 percent wage raise plus other benefits. Within weeks of that settlement John L. Lewis negotiated an agreement with U.S. Steel. It gave recognition to the Steelworkers Union and provided both a 10 percent wage increase and a forty-hour working week. What was so significant about U.S. Steel's capitulation to the workers was that throughout the industrial sector the steel companies had the reputation of being strongly anti-union.

These settlements signalled that the major industries had accepted unions and collective bargaining. Scores of settlements in the United States were soon signed in other industries.

* * *

UNION BREAKTHROUGH IN CANADA

Industrial relations in Canada were very different than in the United States during the 1930s. Militancy was rising as the Depression continued. The Workers Unity League was organizing in all of the big plants, particularly auto and steel. The CCF had been founded in 1933 and many workers were attracted to this more moderate brand of socialism. Canadian workers followed what was going on in the United States. By 1937 the successes in the United States encouraged them to work openly for unions in this country.

The big test was to come at the giant Oshawa, Ontario, General Motors car assembly plant. There had been union organizing in the 1920s, but it had stalled because of conflict between craft and industrial unionization. In late 1936 there were wage cuts while the company posted record profits. In the meantime, the Flint sit-down strike and the organization of the auto and steel industries in the United States showed what could happen with militant action. Oshawa automobile workers were openly talking union.[8]

The UAW headquarters in Detroit sent in an organizer and soon virtually all of the Oshawa workers had joined the union. Negotiations began in March 1937 and by April an agreement had been made between the union local and the company. Then the unexpected happened. Mitch Hepburn, the Liberal Ontario premier, intervened and the negotiations collapsed. A strike began with the objectives of union recognition, an increase in wages, a forty-hour working week, and other benefits.

Hepburn played an active role in the strike. He denounced the union and "foreign agitators." At the same time, he recruited three hundred police officers. (This is the origin of the Ontario Provincial Police.) They were trained in anti-riot tactics, including shooting at the knees of strikers. Despite all the rhetoric and preparation by the police, this was a very peaceful strike with no incidents of violence.

The strike lasted fifteen days and involved most of the workforce, including many women who worked in the upholstery shop at wages much lower than the men's. The police were never used, thanks to the mayor of Oshawa, who would not allow them in the city. The final agreement gave the union virtually all of their demands, but significantly, it did not recognize the UAW. The Oshawa strike was a victory for the union, but it was not a complete victory that led to mass unionization as happened following the Flint sit-down in the United States. The Oshawa local did not get union recognition until 1941; recognition for other auto workers in Ontario would take much longer.

The war for Canadians started in September 1939. Within months unemployment vanished as men and women joined the military, and industry was converted to producing scores of different types of armaments, from rifles and artillery shells to tanks, ships, and airplanes. Government regulations controlled every aspect of industrial life, including unions. There were to be no work stoppages, and no strikes. Union organization continued but unionists were frustrated. Without the possibility of a strike they had little leverage with employers. As the war began to wind down in the summer of 1945, that changed.

In the Windsor Ford plant, the assembly line workers were not happy. They had a local union, but the company stalled negotiations. Just across the Detroit River the workers at the giant River Rouge plant had gained union recognition, better working conditions, and higher wages. The Windsor Ford plant workers wanted the same, but the company refused. Finally, on September 12, 1945, just days after the conclusion of the war, eleven thousand Ford Windsor workers went on strike. Soon the struggle became a test of will. The company was hoping for a return of conditions where they had control over the workforce. The UAW Local 200, which represented the workers, was determined to gain union security.[9]

The strike went on for ninety-nine days. The crisis came around the power plant that supplied heat for the factory. The plant was closed by the strikers and management wanted to open it as winter approached. The union refused. Police were assembling and the threat to break the picket line and the strike was very real. In response the union local formed a car blockade of the power plant stretching twenty blocks. There was little the police could do, and they never did intervene in the strike.

Negotiations resumed, the blockade was removed, and a settlement was reached. On the sensitive issue of union security, it was agreed by both sides to have the issue arbitrated by Justice Ivan Rand. His decision was that workers should not be required to be members of the union, but they must pay union dues because everyone working in the plant benefited from the work of unions. Today this ruling is written into Canadian labour law. It is called the Rand Formula.

The other major event that established the Canadian labour movement after the Second World War was the 1946 Stelco strike in Hamilton.[10] The steel industry had long been anti-union and nowhere in North America was this more the case than at Stelco, led by its president, Hugh Hilton. Steelworkers Local 1005 was established in the late 1930s, but it had no security, the company would not negotiate with its leaders, and before long the effort languished.

As the veterans returned from the war many of them, along with the union activists, knew that this had to change or the union would die. Communists had provided the leadership of the local until the end of the war, but a new union executive was elected, dominated by workers who were CCF members. Negotiating objectives were set: increased wages, a forty-hour week, two weeks of vacation, and a union shop that required all workers pay union dues.

Hilton made it clear that the company would not negotiate. Soon the unionists realized that management was bringing food, bedding, and other essentials into the plant. An airstrip was being prepared inside the Stelco property. The company was planning to keep producing steel to break the strike and the union. Hugh Hilton's comments were front-page news. He called the union leaders communists and said they were spreading lies. He made it clear he would never accept a union in "his plant."

The strike was called for July 15 and the vast majority of workers walked off the job. But a number of workers and students specially recruited stayed inside the plant and were preparing to work for the duration of the strike. They were called "scabs" by the picketers. The estimates of how many stayed inside the plant vary. Some place the number at one thousand.

This was a tactic to break the strike, and it was a real threat to the union. If the company continued producing steel and delivering it to their customers, the strike would be in jeopardy. Soon it became clear the strike would be won or lost on the picket line. The union could not stop the company from producing steel, but if the company could not get it through the picket lines and deliver it to their customers, it would do little good. Every day there were incidents. There was often violence as trucks tried to get through to supply those inside, or when scabs tried to sneak through the fence at night to visit their families. But the picket lines stayed strong and were never broken.

It was a strike fought in the air, by sea, and on land. Leaflets were dropped from union airplanes, union boats were used to harass company boats supplying the plant, and there were scores of skirmishes on the picket lines. Politicians got involved, some denouncing the picketers for being violent, and others, like Hamilton mayor Sam Lawrence, defending them. For a time, it looked like the federal government would intervene by sending in the RCMP to open the picket lines, but it never happened.

Negotiations, in the end, did settle the strike. Hugh Hilton was quietly moved out of the limelight as the company sought a settlement. The union did not win all of its demands but on the important issues it was a union victory. Local 1005 got union security, an increase in pay, and other benefits. This was a dramatic strike, in the full glare of publicity, fought against a determined opponent, and the union had gained a clear victory.

At the conclusion of both the First and the Second World Wars there were strikes and militant actions, but the outcomes could not be more different. In 1919 the Winnipeg General Strike was broken by the government, and it took two decades to recover from the loss. After the Second World War the workers and the unions were much better prepared. The strikes gained union recognition and improved wages and working conditions. It had taken 150 years, but the Canadian trade union movement had finally been established on a firm footing.

* * *

UNIONS TODAY

In the more than seventy years since the recognition of strikes after the Second World War much has changed in the Canadian trade union movement. Unions are more secure. They operate within federal and provincial legislation that structures how collective bargaining is to be conducted, and that has helped to provide more stable relationships between employers, employees, and unions.

By the 1950s virtually all companies, unionized or not, changed the way they dealt with their employees. The bully foreman was retired, and a much more co-operative work environment emerged, where all employees were treated in a more humane way. Companies and industrial relations experts would have us believe these changes were the result of more enlightened attitudes toward workers. That may be partly true, but the real reason for the change was the realization that a more co-operative work environment would lessen conflict and avoid labour militancy and other forms of trouble. The trade union movement played a huge role in creating this new relationship between employees and employers in all places of work, and it continues to have an impact on both unionized and non-unionized workplaces.

The emergence of a more co-operative workplace does not mean that conflict has disappeared. International comparisons show that Canada has very high rates of days lost to labour disputes, both strikes and lockouts. A 2009 study showed we had the highest strike days of all developed countries, much higher than countries like France, Spain, and Britain, which have reputations for having militant unionists.[11]

There are different reasons for this. One is that Canadian industrial relations are modelled after labour legislation in the United States. It is illegal for work stoppages to occur during the life of a contract. That means both labour and management focus on negotiations at the end of the contract. When they fail and a strike or lockout happens, it tends to be long and drawn out until a compromise can emerge.

Another reason is that our industrial relations system is adversarial and conflict-based, pitting unions against management. Other countries like Germany and those in Scandinavia have developed systems that involve workers in management through works councils. Companies are also required to appoint union representatives on corporate boards of directors. This tends to decrease conflict.

Despite our adversarial industrial-relations system, days lost to labour disputes in Canada have been going down since the 1980s.[12] Union activity has always been shaped by changes in the economy and the workforce. The highest point of unionization was in the 1950s. Since then the percentage of the workforce that are members of unions has been slowly decreasing. In 2014 the unionized workforce stood at 31.5 percent. This is considerably higher than in the United States, where it was 11.3 percent in the same year, but lower than in most European countries.

The major change in union membership in Canada has been a decrease in the proportion of private sector workers that are unionized. Today it stands at 17 percent. In the United States it is only 6.7 percent. Manufacturing in the past was at the centre of union activity and militancy, but the number of workers in that sector has been shrinking. In the 1950s about 25 percent of the country's workforce worked in manufacturing, by 2000 it was about 15 percent, and today only 9.2 percent of the workforce is employed in the sector. The reasons are the offshoring of manufacturing to low wage countries and technological change. Some predict the introduction of robots will reduce the manufacturing workforce even more in the future.

The most dramatic growth of unionization in the postwar period has been in the public sector. About 60 percent of all union members in the country work for government, and about 75 percent of the public sector workers are unionized. Virtually all of the rest are in senior management positions. Today it is teachers, health care workers, prison guards, planners, and other federal, provincial, and municipal employees who are at the centre of the movement.

The growth and size of the public sector is the main reason for unionization. By the 1950s the size of government was growing rapidly as activist governments introduced new programs. It is very hard to administer huge bureaucracies. The principle of equity between workers is difficult to maintain. Administrators can get out of control. Grievances, in some departments, mount up. Negotiations are difficult with many different issues and complications.

Top-down administration never works well. The only practical way to manage problems is to empower the workers so that their voices can be heard within the bureaucracy. Giving meaningful representation to workers is what unions do, and that is why unionization spread as the size of government bureaucracies grew. Politicians recognized these issues and there was very little opposition to the unionization of the Canadian public sector.

The rise of public sector unionization is another reason why the numbers of days lost to strikes has been decreasing. It is rare that public sector workers go on strike. Some now are disallowed from striking by legislation because they are deemed to provide essential services.

Quebec is an exception to the rule that public sector workers are less militant. The Common Front Strikes of 1972 were so widespread that some compared it to a general strike. Negotiations had been going on with the public sector in Quebec, and that led to a day of protest on March 28. Then on April 11 about 210,000 provincial sector workers went out on strike and the province ground to a halt. Poorly paid hospital workers were arrested for incidents and jailed and fined. There was more jailing of union leaders, which led to 300,000 workers across the province going on strike. Protests broke out across the province. Radio stations were occupied, factories were seized, and towns were taken over by strikers. In the end the union leaders were released from jail on the condition that they instruct their members to return to work.

The Common Front Strikes were not seen as a defeat by workers in Quebec. On the contrary, the strikes led to greater organization and a very effective union strategy, particularly around public sector negotiations in the province. Unlike in other provinces, the public sector unions in Quebec have played an important role in shaping the provincial politics.

Other than Quebec, the most important political strike in recent years was the Day of Protest strike against wage controls in 1976. On October 14, 1.2 million workers across the country went on a one-day strike, the largest protest by workers ever held in Canada. In response, the federal government cancelled wage controls eight months before they were to end.

Unions have continued to have an impact on Canada, but it is still a movement that has not reached its potential. If there is one major criticism it is that unions have not continued their organizing drives to bring benefits to individuals and families who suffer poverty and a lack of adequate income.

Today, about one-third of the workforce is employed by restaurants, small factories, farms, and in the bush. Some living in poverty are on social assistance, but most work full-time at low paying jobs. A growing number of Canadians now work on contract with no job security and no benefits. (In Toronto, the GTA, and Hamilton, 52 percent of the workforce have temporary, contract, or part-time jobs.) Many companies keep a large part of their workforce as part-time employees so they do not have to pay benefits.

The income inequality that has grown in recent years is partly attributable to these changes in the workforce. In principle, most workers have the right to join unions and benefit from collective bargaining, but in practice employers use anti-union legislation at every occasion. Some employers still resort to bullying, intimidation, and harassment to keep them from joining unions. This can be effective with immigrants, young workers, and minority groups.

The next challenge for unions will be to break through these barriers to provide the benefits of unionization to all workers.

* * *

UNION DEMOCRACY AND PARTICIPATION

"Democracy at the workplace" is an old slogan, and unions have done more to achieve democracy for workers than any other grassroots organization. In the discussions and analysis of unions, it is often ignored that they provide a practical way to empower workers and help to achieve a form of democracy at the workplace.

Unions are decentralized so that union locals represent one workplace, like a factory within a larger corporation, or a unit of government workers. All of the locals collectively make up the union. It is a federated structure. Members of each local elect one of their own workmates to be president of the local and others are elected onto the executive. Stewards and chief stewards are also elected. These are coveted positions, and the workers elected to these union positions are leaders on the shop floor or the office where they work. Except when they are on union business, the executive members of a local continue to work in the plant or the government department. They are workers, just like all of the others.

That means that the leaders of every local union are intimately connected to their workmates. They are accessible; they know what is going on in the shop or office; they understand the problems; they hear the rumours; they know the foreman and the managers. They are also drawn into the politics of the broader union; they go to union meetings at a district and national levels, and know the problems other unionists are facing in other companies and government offices. They understand the management and the broader issues of the union. Above all they are connected with their workmates on the shop floor or in the school or government department where they work.

It is this grassroots democratic union structure that empowers workers and gives them control over the local issues that are important to the members. The leaders of the local are very close to the membership. They can respond immediately to the issues that arise because they know what is going on and are trusted by the people they represent.

Unions have provided a practical way for members to participate at their workplace, in their union, and in the public life of their communities and the country. Trade unions have strengthened our democracy by giving a voice to millions of people. These types of grassroots organizations are essential if we are to build a participatory democracy.

In the mid-1970s I spent a summer researching the politics of Local 1005 of the Steelworkers, which represented the 12,500 workers at the giant Stelco plant in Hamilton.[13] I got to know many of the leaders of the union personally. What struck me about them was their pride in being both a worker in a steel mill and a leader of a strong union. These were not your alienated workers. They made steel, and they were militant unionists, and they were proud of both. They were participating in a movement to help and defend their fellow workers, and that participation helped to give meaning to their lives.

That is grassroots participatory democracy at its best. But there are other organizations like this. We are going to look at co-ops and non-profits next.

CHAPTER 7

CO-OPERATIVES AND THE SOCIAL ECONOMY

Canada's alternative co-operative and non-profit economy, or the "social economy" as it is often called, is thriving. It now accounts for 8.5 percent of the Canadian GDP. That is more than the retail trade, and close to the value of the mining, oil, and gas extraction industry. Two million Canadians are employed in the sector.[1]

The social economy is best described as one made up of non-governmental organizations. It is "the third sector," operating somewhere between private businesses and government. It includes non-profits, charities, co-operatives, credit unions, foundations, and mutual societies — organizations as varied as community-run day care centres, non-profit social service agencies, housing co-ops, and co-operative insurance companies.

Many think the social economy is funded by government, but less than 20 percent of the funds come from that source. Most of that money goes to non-profits delivering medical or social services. Almost all co-operatives are self-sufficient and receive no grants of any kind. They are essentially businesses competing with private sector companies, but they are run democratically by the members. Profits are plowed back into the organization or turned over to the members.

Canada has a very large and active social economy. There is a tradition in this country of working together to solve common problems, or to help others in need. This is an important element of the participatory democratic society that we are building.

It would be almost impossible to describe all of the different elements of this movement. Most are small, successful, self-reliant organizations. This is an account of some of the most interesting and largest of the groups. It focuses on the co-operative movement because it has been around the longest, and is the most varied.

* * *

PRINCIPLES AND TYPES OF CO-OPS

The origins of the co-operative movement go back to 1844 in Britain when a group of workers from the town of Rochdale (today part of Greater Manchester) established a store. This led to the Rochdale Society of Equitable Pioneers and the co-operative movement.[2] Later, groups in Germany and France developed financial co-operatives that were savings and loans organizations. In time seven principles of co-operatives were established that continue to guide co-operatives around the world:[3]

1. 1st Principle: Voluntary and Open Membership

2. 2nd Principle: Democratic Member Control

3. 3rd Principle: Member Economic Participation

4. 4th Principle: Autonomy and Independence

5. 5th Principle: Education, Training, and Information

6. 6th Principle: Co-operation among Co-operatives

7. 7th Principle: Concern for Community

Today there are different types of co-operatives. The financial co-ops include organizations like the caisse populaire, credit unions, and co-operative insurance companies. Farm and fishing co-ops are called producer co-operatives. Worker co-ops are business organizations owned by the workers and operated on co-op principles. Each worker is a member and has a share in the operation and management of the enterprise. Profits, if any, are shared equally. In Quebec there are a number of worker co-ops. Some are small groups of construction workers. Others are restaurants.

Outside of Quebec worker co-ops are rare. Urbane Cycle, a Toronto bicycle repair shop and retail store, is a worker's co-op, as is Just Us! Coffee Roasters Co-op, a fair trade coffee importer, processor, retail shop, and coffee house in Wolfville, Nova Scotia.[4] Just Us! also has a membership category called investor members that have a voice in the running of the co-op.

Consumer co-ops are usually in the food industry. There are a number of large food co-op stores and gas stations in the West and Atlantic Canada. In consumer co-operatives the customers are the members. That means there can be thousands of members, most of whom do not participate in the co-op or the management of the enterprise. Mountain Equipment Co-operative (MEC) is the largest consumer co-op in the country.

Housing co-operatives have a unique history but follow co-op principles. Each building is a co-op. The members are the residents and they manage and maintain the building. Each housing co-op then is a member of a broader co-op federation, usually organized provincially or by a city, like the Co-operative Housing Federation of Toronto.

* * *

THE FARM CO-OPS

It was in the mid-nineteenth century, in rural communities, that the first co-operatives emerged in this country. Mutual insurance companies were established for protection from fire and crop failure. In the 1880s the Knights of Labor established co-op stores, but all of them soon failed. Still, the movement slowly developed in rural Canada. Between 1860 and 1900 some twelve hundred co-op creameries were founded in Ontario and Quebec. Many continue to operate to this day.

By the turn of the twentieth century farmers in Ontario, Quebec, Nova Scotia, and Manitoba had begun establishing marketing and purchasing societies so they could work collectively to get lower prices when they bought items like farm machinery and to get better prices for their produce. They found that by working together they could avoid overpaying merchants.

On the Prairies it was the marketing of grain that led to the most successful farm co-ops. The late Ian MacPherson, the chronicler of Canadian co-operatives, wrote, "The most dramatic co-operative development in Canadian co-operative history occurred in the grain belt during the 1920s with the pooling crusade, which swept the grain producing regions of the Canadian Prairies and influenced the development of co-operatives among other commodity producers both there and in other regions."[5]

As the prairies were settled, farmers learned that they had to work together because they were on isolated farms, and they did not have the money to pay for hired help. By 1911 both Manitoba and Alberta grain grower co-operatives had emerged along with co-operative grain elevator companies. The co-op model interested farmers because it meant working together, something they had long done.

By the 1920s prairie farmers were in trouble from pests like grasshoppers, drought, and rock bottom prices. During the First World War the federal government set a fixed price for wheat, but once the war was over, growers were at the mercy of the market yet again. Some turned to politics and elected Farm Parties provincially, and Progressive candidates federally, but that brought only marginal help.

In 1923 Saskatchewan farmers set out on a campaign to establish a wheat pool co-operative that would store grain, process it, and market it. Everything depended on whether 50 percent of the province's total acreage was pledged to the pool. Anything less was considered insufficient. The campaign turned into a farmers' crusade with enthusiastic public meetings, songs, and growing excitement. Finally, in June 1924 the wheat pool was over the top. As many as 46,500 farmers (51 percent of the total) had pledged their crops to the pool. By 1929 the wheat pool was handling 150 million bushels of wheat a year. It owned one thousand elevators, built fourteen miles apart, along the rail lines, the distance a horse-drawn wagon could travel in a day.

The wheat pool reshaped politics in Saskatchewan. It was part of the rise of populism reflected in the Progressive and Farm Parties. The belief in co-ops contributed to the foundation of the CCF in 1933, and the party took its name from the movement: Co-operative Commonwealth Federation. The election of the first CCF government in 1944 in Saskatchewan was led by Tommy Douglas.

Farmers were attracted to co-operatives because the movement was a combination of individual enterprise and pragmatic co-operation. It was built on community. Churches played an important role in building trust and friendships. Farmers had always worked together at harvest and in time of emergencies. Co-ops were a natural outgrowth of those community networks.

Today co-operatives continue to be strong in rural Canada. More than one thousand continue to operate, even though the number of people involved in farming has shrunk. New specialized farm co-ops have been developed to market products like goat's milk. Organic farmers across the country are forming co-ops to market their produce directly to consumers. Rural co-ops have a bright future; however, the wheat pools that were once was the prime proselytizer of the co-op message on the Prairies have passed out of existence.

* * *

ALPHONSE DESJARDINS AND THE CAISSE POPULAIRE

On December 1, 1900, Alphonse Desjardins, his wife Dorimène, and 130 residents of Lévis, Quebec, met and founded the Caisse Populaire de Quebec. This was the first caisse, or credit union, in North America. Today credit unions are the foundation of the co-operative financial institutions that now spread across North America, and the Desjardins Movement that has grown from that first meeting in Lévis is by far the largest and most successful.

Alphonse Desjardins was a middle-class *fonctionnaire*, as he would be called by Québécois today, who worked as a stenographer for governments in both Quebec City and Ottawa. In 1897, he was in a parliamentary committee meeting and heard testimony about usurious rates of interest being charged farmers and working people. One example was of a farmer who borrowed $150 and by the time the loan was discharged had paid $5,000. Desjardins was shocked, alarmed, and determined to do something about it.

For the next three years he studied finances and credit institutions. Then he focused on financial co-operatives that were then emerging in France and Germany and corresponded with a number of the European leaders of that movement. Once he understood the benefits of the co-operative model of financial institutions, he went ahead and founded the Lévis caisse populaire.

The location of the first caisse was in the Desjardins home in Lévis, a modest white wooden house that is still standing. Today it operates as a museum commemorating the family and the humble origins of the

Desjardins movement. Dorimène, Alphonse's wife and the mother of their ten children, operated the caisse in its first years. The original leger books, showing deposits as small as ten cents, are on display.

Alphonse and Dorimène worked together. By 1906 special legislation was passed in the Quebec Legislative Assembly and caisse populaires received legal recognition. The Desjardins were devout Catholics and had close associations with the Church. Priests played an important role in promoting the cause. Many of the first caisses were located in parish halls and are still there to this day. The movement spread rapidly through rural Quebec because there were virtually no other financial institutions. In Montreal and other large centres, the movement took longer to establish.

In 1908 Alphonse made his first trip to the United States. At that time many French Canadians were moving to New England to work in textile mills and other factories. He helped groups establish savings and loans co-operatives in New Hampshire, the first credit unions in the United States. He went on to Ontario, where he helped to establish the Civil Service Savings and Loans Society, a financial co-op for federal civil servants. Today it has become the Alterna Credit Union, one of the largest in Ontario. By 1912 he founded the first caisse populaire in Ontario to serve francophones. By the time of his death in 1920 Alphonse Desjardins had helped to found 132 caisses in Quebec, 19 in Ontario, and 9 in the United States.

Today the Desjardins Movement is a full-fledged financial institution offering savings accounts, loans to individuals and companies, insurance, and other financial services. There are 750 caisse populaires managed by independent boards with 6,000 elected board members. Each caisse is independent. The board hires the manager and runs the caisse, but they operate under an increasingly centralized set of rules and guidelines administered by Desjardins central. Altogether they have 42,000 employees. In 2015 Desjardins had total assets of $248 billion. In Quebec, it is larger than any of the Canadian banks.

* * *

FISHING CO-OPS

At about the same time that farm co-ops and credit unions were developing, fishermen on both the east and west coasts of Canada were forming their own co-operative associations. Farm and fishing co-ops are called *producer co-operatives* because they produce a product like wheat or dried salt cod; the producers work together through the co-op to market the product, cut out the middleman, and keep as much profit as possible.

On both coasts the problem was similar. In Newfoundland and the Maritime provinces, merchants would extend credit to the fishermen to help get them through the winter and to buy gear for the next season. The fishermen, then, would be obliged to sell their catch to the merchant at low prices. Sometimes the fishermen never saw cash. They were always in debt. In British Columbia it was a similar system only it was the canneries who extended the credit and forced the fishermen to sell their catch to them at low prices to eliminate the debt.

It was in Newfoundland, then a British colony and not a part of Canada, that the fishermen first rebelled. In November 1908 a group founded the Fishermen's Protective Union, which worked like a co-operative. They established stores in outports that purchased fish for cash and sold fishing gear and other necessities without a markup. At its height the Protective Union had twenty-one thousand members and 206 councils, more than half of the fishermen in Newfoundland.[6]

By 1912 the Fishermen's Protective Union became active in politics. They adopted a manifesto calling for radical changes in fisheries policies and various social policies such as old age benefits. The next year a group of fishermen from the union ran for office and eight of their members were elected. For the next two decades they played a role in government, usually in coalition with other political parties. The party passed out of existence in 1934 when responsible government was suspended by the British. The Protective Union remained in existence until 1977 when they faced bankruptcy and sold their ten remaining stores.

The Protective Union ultimately failed financially, but it had a huge impact on the lives of Newfoundland fishermen and their families. It ended the virtual stranglehold that merchants had on the industry and improved the living standards across the province. Newfoundland fishermen remain militant and continue to defend their interests through collective organizations like the Fish, Food and Allied Workers Union.

The origins of fishermen's co-ops on the west coast is traced to the time the Finns settled the village of Sointula on Malcolm Island. They had come to British Columbia to be farmers and in 1908 they formed the Sointula Co-operative Association. Farming did not work out very well. The soil was poor and the community was too far away from markets. Many of them decided to go into fishing, but they did not have the money for boats and gear. Like others, they went to the cannery companies for loans, and found that they had to market their fish to them at low prices to pay off the debt.

This did not sit well with the Sointula Finns. They had a tradition of working together through co-ops. Soon they began to organize other fishermen like the Japanese, who made up a large part of the industry, and other groups. In 1929 the British Columbia Fishermen's Co-operative Association was formed.[7]

With the onset of the Depression the co-op collapsed, but by that time the power of the canneries was broken. Today there is not just one fisherman's co-operative on the west coast but several. Each one is independent, but they help one another when needed.

Today the Sointula Finns on Malcolm Island continue to support and build their co-ops. They have a co-op store, a credit union, a tree planters' co-op, a shellfish co-op, and most recently a food co-op.

On the east coast things were not getting any better. In Nova Scotia the fishing industry had fallen into chronic decline by the late 1920s. The social conditions in fishing communities were bad. Poverty was widespread. The federal government was concerned but nobody seemed to know what to do about it. At about the same time St. Francis Xavier University in Antigonish established an extension department and appointed Moses Coady, a Catholic priest, to head it. The Canadian government asked Father Coady to help organize the fishermen.[8]

As the Depression set in, bad social conditions became dire. Coady approached the multitude of problems in scores of communities through education. He and his fellow educators set up study clubs and leadership courses that helped people understand their situation. Soon the clubs and associations began to launch co-operative business ventures in a number of different fields, from fish canning, marketing, dairy, housing, and agriculture.

The most important development was establishing credit unions. Coady did not turn to the Desjardins Movement for help. He went to the United States. Curiously Alphonse Desjardins had gone to the United States to help them set up their first credit unions, and now the favour was being repaid as Americans came to Nova Scotia to help them set up credit unions.

Coady's unique approach came to be called the Antigonish Movement. People learned appropriate skills, which helped them diagnose the problems. Then they found the right kind of organizations, like co-ops and credit unions, that could help solve the problems. It was self-help through education.

By the end of the 1930s the reputation of Father Moses Coady had spread from Nova Scotia across North America. He was a powerful speaker who inspired thousands of people. His message was that practical education can help people to help themselves through organizations like co-operatives and credit unions.

Today the co-operative movement remains a vital force across Atlantic Canada in both Acadian and English-speaking communities. St. Francis Xavier University continues its adult education programs through the Coady International Institute. They take a "transformational approach to learning" that emphasizes the empowerment of people. That, they believe, is the key to social change. Many of the students of the Institute come from the developing world.

* * *

NON-PROFITS

Non-profits are closely allied to co-ops, but they have a different structure and objectives. They are almost always organized democratically with a board elected from the membership. They include organizations like foundations, associations, arts service organizations, health care service groups, social service organizations, and recreational groups. Some are very large, like the YMCA. Canadian non-profits are growing in size and number of employees working in the sector.

The main distinction between non-profits and co-ops is around profits. Most co-ops are for-profit organizations. They compete in the marketplace. Any profits are distributed to the owners or members. Non-profits, as the name suggests, are specifically set up to provide services but not to make a profit.

* * *

HOUSING CO-OPERATIVES AND NON-PROFITS

When people talk about co-ops in cities like Toronto and Vancouver they almost always mean housing co-operatives. They have been one of the most successful social programs ever developed in this country, and they continue to make a major contribution to the lives of many people.[9]

The first housing co-ops go back as far as 1913 when they were built as student housing. In the 1930s the Antigonish Movement in Nova Scotia organized workers to build housing using their own labour and skill, and after they were finished the houses were sold to members of the co-op.

Public housing was built after the Second World War, but by the 1960s it was criticized as poor people's ghettos that led to major social problems. A group of social activists came together and lobbied the federal government, arguing that what was needed was mixed income housing. Finally, a comprehensive program along those lines was established in 1973.

The new affordable housing program was not just for co-operative housing. Some was built as non-profit housing, sponsored by churches, trade unions, or community groups. The co-operative housing sector quickly organized to meet the federal government requirements, and local co-op housing groups emerged across the country, including Quebec. They delivered an excellent program.

The only way that affordable housing can be built in this country is with government financial support to reduce the costs of acquiring the land and of building. Federal support came in the form of preferential mortgages, operating subsidies, and assistance to low-income households with their rent. The public investment came back to the government as the mortgages were paid off. The housing co-op or non-profit organizations took responsibility for buying the land, contracting the architects and builders, and managing the project from beginning to end.

The government does not own the co-operatives or non-profits. They are independent corporations that work in partnership with government. In the co-operatives, each building, or sometimes group of buildings, makes up one co-op. These are rental buildings that are run democratically. All residents are members of the co-op and are responsible for managing the day-to-day operations. There are regular elections for the co-op board. Between 25 percent and 30 percent of the residents are low-income and receive assistance with rent payments. The rest of the residents pay market rent. The co-op housing built under this program is mixed income and democratically controlled.

This program ran from 1973 to 1992, when it was terminated by the federal government. Ontario continued supporting co-ops until 1995. British Columbia had a modest program until 2001. Only Quebec continues its affordable housing program, but even it has been scaled back because of a lack of funds. Today there are hundreds of housing co-ops across Canada, mainly in the cities, with ninety-four thousand units housing a quarter of a million people. The level of satisfaction among residents is very high.

Meanwhile the lack of affordable housing, particularly in the large cities like Toronto and Vancouver, has become a crisis today. We need a good affordable housing program, and the co-ops and non-profits provide an excellent model.

* * *

ARCTIC CO-OPERATIVES LIMITED

During the 1960s in the Canadian North people were moving off the land into small communities. The market for furs was disappearing and the Hudson's Bay stores were closing. The way of life of the people was changing, and they had to adapt. Gradually what emerged to deal with some of these issues was a network of co-ops organized under the broader federation called Arctic Co-operatives Limited.[10]

Help to organize the co-ops came from French Catholic priests and other southerners trusted by the people, but the co-ops have always been led by northerners. There are two major groups: the Inuit in the far North, and the Dene people in the Northwest Territories.

Co-ops were a natural way for doing business in the North because people had always worked together to solve their problems. Some of the earliest co-ops were developed for the marketing of art and handicrafts. But the major problem for the people, after they began living in settled communities, was getting supplies of food and other necessities.

Today retail stores are at the heart of the co-op movement in the North. Altogether there are thirty-two community-based co-operatives located in

Nunavut, the Northwest Territories, and the Yukon. They sell food, clothing, snowmobiles, gasoline, and a host of other items. Recently some of the co-ops have built small hotels for visitors and the growing tourist trade. Fishing is important in some communities, and the co-op network organizes the sale of arctic char and turbot in the south.

Arctic Co-operatives Ltd., the federated organization whose members are the community-based co-ops, has its headquarters in Winnipeg. The member co-ops order what they need and the staff of Arctic Co-operatives do the buying and shipping. This helps to keep the costs down. Winnipeg supplies the member co-ops in the eastern Arctic and a group in Edmonton supplies the western Arctic. There is a transportation subsidy from the federal government, but the cost of all items in the North is still very high.

Leadership has been key to making this organization work and that has come primarily from the members in the communities. There are regular meetings where delegates from the community co-ops come together to talk about problems and make decisions. There are different languages and dialects spoken in the North. English has become the language used in the co-op network became it is now spoken by most of the people in the North.

Altogether there are about a thousand people employed in the network. It has become an organization in which many people have learned business skills that they use in other parts of their lives. A number of the political leaders of the three territories have either been active members of co-ops or have worked for a co-op in the North.

*   *   *

CO-OP ATLANTIC

Co-operatives have long been active and viable in Atlantic Canada and today the leader in the region is Co-op Atlantic. It works in all four Atlantic provinces in both French and English. Its headquarters is in Moncton, New Brunswick.[11]

Co-op Atlantic is a federated co-operative with 128 member co-ops that operate in a number of different sectors. In agriculture they provide a wide number of services from feed programs for animals to products that produce higher crop yields. Member co-ops operate gas stations and deliver home heating fuel.

Their real estate division develops retail facilities and condominiums. It manages homes for seniors and people with special needs and has developed nineteen hundred homes that are both market-based and social housing.

The Acadian communities in Atlantic Canada are very involved in the co-operative movement. The small town of Cheticamp, Nova Scotia, on the east coast of Cape Breton Island, for example, has a co-op grocery store that also sells Acadian handicrafts, a co-op restaurant, a co-op radio station, Cheticamp Housing Co-operative, and a caisse populaire.

* * *

VANCITY CREDIT UNION

Vancity is a credit union that offers full financial services with fifty-nine branches in Metro Vancouver, the Fraser Valley, Victoria, Squamish, and Alert Bay. It has 519,000 member owners and 2,500 employees. It was founded in 1946 and now has $19.8 billion in assets.[12]

The credit union has long had a progressive reputation for ethical investing and as a good employer. It was the first financial institution in Canada to offer mortgages to women without a male co-signer. It has a mutual fund that invests only in carbon neutral companies. It is Canada's largest "living wage" employer, paying its employees an hourly wage required for two working parents to meet the needs of a family of four.

Vancity has a record of investing in affordable housing, community development in aboriginal communities, supporting organic and locally grown food outlets, clean energy, and various other social enterprises.

* * *

MOUNTAIN EQUIPMENT CO-OP

Mountain Equipment Co-op (MEC) is interesting because it espouses a new set of environmental values of sustainability and yet still retains the values of service to community and democracy.[13]

Founded in 1971 by a group of Vancouver-based mountain climbers and outdoor enthusiasts, the chain has now grown to twenty-one stores right across Canada: five in B.C., three in Alberta, six in Ontario, five in Quebec, and one each in Manitoba and Nova Scotia. It has four million members, more than any other co-op in the country.

Environmental sustainability is very serious concern to them. This is what they say on their website: "We want MEC and our members to set examples that inspire other organizations and individuals toward environmental, social, and economic sustainability."

This approach is repeated in many different ways by the organization. The MEC stores are modern, attractive, and built to sustainable standards. They sell equipment that is high quality but affordable in price. Some of the profits, or saved earnings as they might call it, are given away to environmental causes, or property is purchased to preserve it for outdoor activities.

The staff are knowledgeable about the equipment and many are active in sports and outdoor activities. MEC leaders impress on the employees and the members that they are not there to make a profit, but to serve the community who want to enjoy nature, protect the environment, and promote outdoor activities and lifestyles. Social responsibility and environmental sustainability are fundamental to their message.

Even their relationship with their suppliers reflects their values. Sport apparel sold in MEC stores is in most cases designed by their own employees and manufactured by contractors in Canada, Europe, China, and other countries. MEC requires suppliers to sign a code of standards on work, safety, and human rights to ensure that the workers are treated fairly.

Another new co-op that has been shaped by environmental concerns is Solar Share.

* * *

SOLAR SHARE

Solar Share is Canada's leading renewable energy co-operative. It was founded in 2002 and operates in Ontario. This is an investor's co-op that has eleven hundred members. The motivation of the investors is to be part of the green revolution, working to stop, or slow climate change, and at the same time earn a solid return on their investment.[14]

Solar Share is modelled on the alternative energy co-ops in Denmark and Germany. Danish co-operatives have installed 86 percent of the wind turbines in that country. In Canada alternative energy co-ops were slow to develop. Ontario is ahead of other provinces because of a more favourable provincial environment policy and the Green Energy Act.

Solar Share began life as Wind Share because of its efforts to produce energy from wind turbines. A single windmill was built on the CNE grounds in Toronto, but since that time the co-op wind projects have been stalled because they do not have access to the grid. At that point efforts shifted to solar-based energy production.

The specialty of Solar Share has become installing solar panels on the roofs of industrial and public buildings. These are huge open spaces with no trees or other buildings blocking the sun, and the buildings have good access to the grid. To date the co-op has completed thirty-four projects that produce a very respectable five megawatts of power valued at over $30 million. However, it is still relatively small. The Pickering nuclear power plant, by comparison, produces 3,100 megawatts of power.

The potential for co-operative alternative energy projects is enormous. Solar Share has shown that investors have a great appetite for these types of investments because it gives them a practical way to make a contribution toward a solution to the crisis of climate change by producing electricity environmentally. Now that new electric storage systems are being installed, it will stimulate even more demand for alternative energy.

Co-operative, democratically controlled energy projects provide a way to have ownership and control that produces local jobs and investment returns in the community. At the same time, they will help us meet our goal of reducing greenhouse gas emissions. Across Canada, co-op groups are following the lead of Solar Share. Energy co-ops that will benefit communities and build sustainability have been formed in most provinces.

* * *

THE QUEBEC CO-OP MOVEMENT

The co-op movement in the English-speaking Canadian provinces is impressive, but it is not nearly as large or as important as the movement in Quebec. That province has 40 percent or more of all co-op activity in Canada while having only 23.6 percent of the Canadian population. The Desjardins Movement provides over 50 percent of the co-operative financial activity in the country. The question is, why have co-ops been so successful in that province?

There are different explanations. Quebecers are much more communitarian than English Canadians. They have a strong sense of the importance of community. Some argue that this is a conservative value that comes out of the Catholic Church. Regardless of the reasons, what those values have done is to make co-operatives an economic strategy that remains very attractive to Québécois because it provides local community control.

Everywhere in rural Quebec there are co-ops, and they are prominent even in the large cities of Montreal, Quebec City, and Sherbrooke. In Quebec there are about 3,500 co-operatives compared to 5,000 in the rest of Canada. There are far more Desjardins caisse populaires than branches of banks. The non-financial co-ops alone have 1.4 million members and 28,000 employees. There is a growing number of worker co-ops, particularly in the forestry sector. Large co-ops dominate agriculture. There are consumer co-ops, and the schools give courses on co-operatives. There are scores of housing co-ops and even co-op funeral homes. Many of the health care facilities in the province are organized as co-ops, including one for ambulance drivers. Even a ski centre is organized as a co-op.

In a new development, workers in private companies are joining with management to create a co-op called Co-operative of Employee Shareholders. They are organizations of company workers that purchase shares in the company. That provides more capital for the company and a profit for the workers on investments, but it also gives the employees more power because they can vote those shares as a block.

Now even the Quebec government has joined the effort to strengthen the co-op sector. They have set aside a $140 million fund specifically for investments in co-operatives. The reason the government has done this is because, although co-ops are more difficult to establish than private companies, they have a much better chance of survival. In a province that has an unemployment rate of 8 percent or more that is a powerful incentive.

Political and economic control has long been an important issue in Canada. Across the country there has been a concern that we have become a branch plant economy dominated by American corporations. In Quebec this issue has been particularly important because many are concerned that their province's economy, politics, and culture will be dominated and overwhelmed by the huge Anglo population of North America (both in the United States and English-speaking Canada).

The political slogan *maîtres chez nous* (masters in our own house) emerged in the Quiet Revolution and is an expression of that concern. The separatist struggle was one result of this desire of Québécois to be masters of their own house, and the co-operative movement was another. Co-ops were a practical way that people could build an economy that was democratic and locally controlled. That in turn would make the province more politically and culturally secure.

In recent years the demand for separation in Quebec has been on the wane. The co-operative movement is not the only reason for this, but it has helped Quebecers feel that they have the ability to save their culture and their unique way of life, and to become masters in their own house.

* * *

CO-OPS AND DEMOCRACY

In a capitalist country where most organizations are run on for-profit principles, co-operatives are unique. They are grassroots businesses run on democratic principles. Members and staff participate in the running of the co-ops, and in return they share in the benefits.

Not surprisingly, people who work for co-ops have better wages and higher job satisfaction than employees who work for comparable private-sector companies. Co-op residents and customers feel the same. These are social enterprises run by people who have pooled their resources in an effort to help their communities. It is only natural that those involved feel a sense of satisfaction from their efforts. Co-ops and non-profits are grassroots democratic organizations run by their members and which encourage participation. They are an important part of the participatory democracy that is emerging in Canada.

The co-op movement even reaches out to others in the developing world. The Canadian Co-operative Association is part of an international effort to bring the co-op message to people in countries in need, and to aid in the development of co-ops in these countries by providing expertise and financial help.[15]

What people in the co-op movement understand is that by participating and working together they can solve problems and live more fulfilling lives. That is a powerful message of hope.

CHAPTER 8

THE ENVIRONMENTAL MOVEMENT

Environmentalism has become the most effective grassroots movement of our time. International in scope, it has had an unprecedented impact on governments, corporate business practices, and the way we understand nature, and it is even challenging our way of life in the developed and developing world.

This is a movement based on a commitment to save our planet from the ravages of pollution, over development, and economic growth. It is a mixture of science, idealism, and political action on the streets and in the boardrooms and corridors of political power. What is more, the movement has made an important, even essential contribution to our democracy.

* * *

THE SILENT SPRING

The origins of the movement go back to those who believed in the conservation of nature, a prominent group that had influence up until the 1960s. Conservationists attempted to conserve nature in its pristine form in parks to protect wildlife, particularly rare species, and to stop the worst ravages of industry. Some of the strongest conservationists were hunters and anglers.

The start of the environmental movement as we know it today was the publication of *Silent Spring* by Rachel Carson in 1962. She was a marine biologist and became a popular writer who interpreted science for general readers. *Silent Spring* became a bestseller and was serialized in the *New Yorker.*[1] It became a must-read for a generation of people.

The focus of the book was the impact of human activity on the environment. Carson took an ecological approach that used the idea of the balance of nature and linked it to issues like public health. She questioned modernity, consumerism, and the myth of economic growth as the basis of prosperity.

Silent Spring described the impact of resource exploitation and industrial agriculture on species. The effects of acid rain on forests, and of the pesticide DDT on wildlife, were featured. Air and water pollution were detailed in her book, along with concerns about nuclear waste, carbon dioxide emissions, and the chemical content in processed foods. All of this was carefully documented and backed up by research.

Once the book became popular, corporations began to attack the research and its conclusions. That only increased the attention it received. Governments responded slowly. The greatest impact was with the general public. There were increased concerns about the effect of air and water pollution on the natural world.

* * *

GROWTH OF THE MOVEMENT

There were a number of reasons why environmentalism caught the imagination of the public in the late 1960s. There was a shift away from the conformity of the period after the Second World War. The counter culture movement was having an impact on young people. The peace movement was growing, and opposition to the war in Vietnam became a huge issue. In the United States the civil rights movement, led by Reverend Martin Luther King Jr., galvanized the attention of millions. The environmental movement grew along with the others, so that by the end of the decade it was a major force in the developed world, including Canada.

Educated young people were the early converts, but the environmental message had an impact on the whole population because it confirmed the observations and fears of many that the air was fouled by smoke from factories and refineries, that pristine rivers and lakes were polluted, and that all species of wildlife were threatened.

There was some early action. The Canadian government banned DDT in 1969 and the wildlife population began to recover. There was talk about acid rain and by the 1980s an agreement was signed by the U.S. and Canadian governments to reduce sulfur dioxide emissions.

The real action was the growth of the environmental movement. Many different environmental groups that we know today were established then. Pollution Probe was founded in 1969. They led the fight against DDT and the effort to clean up Lake Erie, which was badly polluted with algae blooms created by phosphorus that came from agricultural runoff.[2]

In 1971 Greenpeace was founded in Vancouver. It was a militant organization that operated in both the environmental and peace movements. Their first action was to try and stop the United States from detonating a nuclear bomb in Alaska. They rented a fishing boat and tried to sail into the blast zone. The resulting publicity turned the group into a huge organization. Greenpeace still has a reputation of militant activism. They have opposed the seal hunt, unsustainable fishing, and the clear cutting of forests, and have been active in anti-nuclear campaigns. By 1985 they had become an international organization with one million members. Today they have 2.8 million.[3]

Over the years there have been a number of other important environmental groups founded in Canada. The Pembina Institute was established in 1984 in Alberta. Today it operates across Canada and focuses on clean energy.[4] The David Suzuki Foundation was founded in 1990.[5] There are a number of local groups in cities across the country that promote and support issues like transit, bike lanes, and recycling. The Toronto Environmental Alliance is the largest. GoodWork.ca lists all of the environmental organizations in Canada. Today there are more than seventy names on the list.[6]

* * *

THE INTERNATIONAL ENVIRONMENTAL MOVEMENT

Internationally the environmental movement became a major force, influencing politics around the world. The first Earth Day in 1970 attracted ten million people in North America alone. In 1972 the U.N. Conference on the Human Environment was held in Stockholm. In 1972 the Club of Rome published *The Limits to Growth,* a book arguing that the planet could not sustain the rate of growth of population, industry, pollution, food production, and resource depletion. In 1973 E.F. Schumacher published *Small Is Beautiful,* an international bestseller. Other conferences and publications followed.

By the 1970s the nuclear industry was under attack. The start of the concern was around the testing of nuclear weapons. Soon the issues around the industry came to include the handling of nuclear waste, uranium mining, and radioactive spills. The meltdown at the Three Mile Island Nuclear Generating Station in Pennsylvania happened in 1979, the Chernobyl accident in 1986. Even feature films explored this issue. *The China Syndrome* was released in 1979 and *Silkwood* in 1986.

The optimism of the environmental movement led to the founding of the Canadian Green Party in 1983. Their aims include eliminating pollution and promoting alternative energy, green industries, and environmental sustainability. Today there are one hundred Green Parties worldwide.

* * *

GOVERNMENT INACTION

At first there appeared to be action to curb pollution by Canadian governments. In 1971 the federal government passed the Clean Air Act; in 1972 it passed the Canada Water Act. The International Great Lakes Water Quality Agreement was signed by Canada and the United States in 1972. In Canada, anti-pollution legislation was passed by the provinces and regulatory agencies were set up.

But the appearance of action proved to be deceiving. Economic growth continued. There was little enforcement of the legislation, and the enforcement that did happen was erratic. Municipalities like Vancouver and Victoria continued to dump raw sewage into the ocean. In Ontario companies like Inco in Sudbury were resistant to air pollution controls, and the government backed off enforcing its own laws.

By the 1990s Canada was seen as a laggard in the worldwide effort to cut pollution. One international study of developed countries ranked Canada twenty-fourth of twenty-five countries in efforts to combat pollution. Only the United States ranked lower. The reasons were poor leadership and lack of political will. Canada, like the United States, favoured business interests over protection of the environment. Government strategy was to pass laws and sign international agreements, but ignore them.

In trade talks the federal government supported clauses in the new agreements that would give corporations the right to challenge governments that passed laws or regulations that threatened private investments. The intent was to make it difficult to pass environmental laws. Maude Barlow and the Council of Canadians played a leading role in using the internet to stop this practice. France in 1998 said it would not support an agreement with such clauses.

By the beginning of the new century the effort to meet the challenge of pollution was in disarray in North America. In the United States the Christian right saw pollution controls as a left-wing plot. President George W. Bush had little interest in the environment. Conservatism was dominant in politics. The interest was in fighting terrorism, the invasions of Iraq and Afghanistan, lowering taxes, increasing economic growth, and increasing profits.

In Canada conservatism had affected the environmental movement even earlier. The Mike Harris government in Ontario cut spending on the environment in 1995. In Ottawa the Chrétien government came to power in Ottawa in 1993. They slashed environmental programs and reduced spending so they could balance the budget. Little effort was made to reduce pollution or to deal with other environmental concerns.

In 2002 the World Summit on Sustainable Development was held in Johannesburg, South Africa. It was boycotted by the United States, and that won the praise of various conservative organizations. Various commitments to reduce energy consumption and overfishing were made, but little happened.

* * *

CLIMATE CHANGE

It has long been known that the burning of fossil fuels — first coal and more recently oil and gas — produces greenhouse gas (GHG) emissions, which are raising temperatures around the globe. It has also long been known that the only way increasing temperatures can be stopped or reduced is by reducing GHG emissions.

This was controversial and an enormous challenge because of the import-ance and wealth of the energy industry, but the international community agreed that something must be done. In 1997 the Kyoto Protocol was signed. The protocol was to come into force in 2005 with the first period of reduc-tions of fossil fuel consumption starting in 2008 and ending in 2012. After that there would be other agreements setting other targets. In the first round, the greatest reductions were to be made by developed countries. The reason was that historically they were responsible for the current levels of greenhouse gases in the atmosphere. After that the reduction targets would be more evenly balanced (something that was to be agreed on at a later date).

Needless to say, all this was very controversial, but the biggest problem was that the two largest producers of GHG emissions (the United States and China) were not even part of the negotiations at Kyoto and had no intention of signing. The Chrétien government, in power in Ottawa at the time, did sign, but did nothing to live up to the conditions in the agreement. Canada was to reduce emissions by 6 percent by 2012, compared to 1990 levels. By 2012 emissions had increased by 24.1 percent.

In 2011 it was announced by the Harper Conservative government that Canada was withdrawing from the Kyoto Protocol. For many, this confirmed Canada's growing reputation as the bad boy of the international community, unwilling to work with other countries to address serious global issues. This damaged the country's international image.

Climate change has become the most difficult environmental issue that we face, and the one that will be the most difficult to solve. As the issue gained prominence, a group of climate change deniers emerged to say that the evidence was not conclusive, or that there was doubt in the scientific community that greenhouse gas emissions were linked to climate change. In both the United States and Canada the climate change deniers were mainly right-wing political operators. They were supported by the oil and gas indus-try and the automobile companies, who had a lot to lose if legislation was passed to cut back on GHG emissions.

The media, particularly right-wing television broadcasters, would report on new studies on climate change, but immediately afterwards they would feature deniers who would repeat that it was not proven conclusively. There can be no doubt that this influenced the debate and made it much more difficult to bring about measures that would lead to the decrease of emissions. Later it was proven that the oil and gas industries were funding the research of climate change deniers.[7]

In 2013 the Intergovernmental Panel on Climate Change published its findings and finally this issue was put to rest.[8] This panel of eminent scientists from several countries showed conclusively that human activity was the major cause of climate change, and if something drastic was not done it would lead to very serious consequences. No longer could there be a backroom cabal of powerful corporate and political interests that could deny climate change.

Finally, in 2015 the Paris Agreement was signed; it committed nations to an action plan to reduce greenhouse gas emissions, and the climate change debate (it appears) has been put to rest. It was the United States, under the leadership of Barack Obama, that made the agreement possible. He brought not only the United States onside, but also China and other major countries. The government of Justin Trudeau changed Canada's environmental policy and our prime minister played an important role in accepting the Paris Agreement.

Canada now is firmly committed to reducing GHG emissions and playing a role in meeting the crisis of climate change. Provinces, and even cities, have stepped forward to play a role. Ontario and Quebec have established a cap and trade policy, and British Columbia has put a tax on carbon emissions. The federal government has announced a plan to set a minimum carbon tax that will increase to $50-per-tonne on carbon emissions by 2022. All revenue raised by that tax will be returned to the provinces.

It remains to be seen whether the provinces will accept the federal plan, or how effective it will be. There is still resistance from businesses. But, clearly, the fight against pollution, environmental degradation, and climate change has gained new momentum in Canada and internationally. Now this is under threat, however.

The election of Donald Trump as U.S. president has thrown all of these efforts in doubt. Trump is a climate change denier. During the election he said that climate change was an attempt by China to harm the United States. There is no evidence that this is true. But his election has made those who have tried to control pollution extremely nervous.

* * *

THE ENVIRONMENTAL MOVEMENT TODAY

It might be expected that the environmental movement would have been damaged from the bruising political events of recent years, but that has not happened. Groups across Canada are still very active and they speak with authority on issues. Today they are playing a larger role in public issues.

The latest group that has emerged goes by the name of the Leap Manifesto. It links the environmental crisis with the movement of aboriginal people and others seeking economic justice. Their campaign promises to put these and other issues at the centre of political life in the future. The group is supported by political, environmental, and aboriginal leaders in the country. The two key leaders are Naomi Klein, an activist and writer, and Avi Lewis, a filmmaker and member of the most prominent family of New Democrats.

The Leap Manifesto expresses a radical and ideological message. The words of the manifesto provide the best explanation of their position.[9]

> We start from the premise that Canada is facing the deepest crisis in recent memory.
>
> We could live in a country powered entirely by renewable energy, woven together by accessible public transit, in which the jobs and opportunities of this transition are designed to systematically eliminate racial and gender inequality. Caring for one another and caring for the planet could be the economy's fastest growing sectors. Many more people could have higher wage jobs with fewer work hours, leaving us ample time to enjoy our loved ones and flourish in our communities.
>
> We know that the time for this great transition is short. Climate scientists have told us that this is the decade to take decisive action to prevent catastrophic global warming. That means small steps will no longer get us where we need to go.
>
> As an alternative to the profit-gouging of private companies and the remote bureaucracy of some centralized

state ones, we can create innovative ownership structures: democratically run, paying living wages and keeping much-needed revenue in communities. And Indigenous Peoples should be first to receive public support for their own clean energy projects. So should communities currently dealing with heavy health impacts of polluting industrial activity.

Power generated this way will not merely light our homes but redistribute wealth, deepen our democracy, strengthen our economy and start to heal the wounds that date back to this country's founding.

The Canadian environmental movement is at the centre of the most important issue facing our country today. In recent years the participation of environmentalists has been a vital contribution to the emerging participatory democracy movement.

CHAPTER 9

COMMUNITY GROUPS

Community groups are incredibly varied, with different objectives, operations, and tactics, but they are not like any of the other movements we have looked at. These groups operate in the sphere of politics, usually local politics. Unlike unions or environmental organizations, there is no unifying ideology or objective that shapes all community groups, other than the principle that they have the right to participate in the political decisions. They are drawn from people of all political parties, religions, and ethnicities.

There are scores of community groups in Canadian cities, suburbs, small towns, and rural areas. With no exaggeration, thousands of groups operate in neighbourhoods across Canada, and they are playing an increasingly important role in the political life of our country. They are among the most dynamic grassroots democratic organizations active today.

The issues that community groups engage in usually spring out of neighbourhood concerns. Sometimes they are so local that they only affect a small group of people. More typically, the issue threatens a whole neighbourhood, and sometimes it is of concern to a whole city the size of Toronto.

A community group will suddenly emerge when an issue becomes controversial, and then disappear just as quickly when the issue is resolved. Other groups will adopt a formal structure. They become incorporated with a constitution, elected officers, a bank account, and formal meetings run by Robert's Rules of Order. Groups like this can be active for years, even generations.[1]

In many cases the groups can be described as opposition organizations. They may oppose a new proposal made by a private developer or government agency that threatens their community. At other times citizen groups become a type of neighbourhood council, monitoring what happens in their community. Others promote certain types of development that they see as beneficial in their neighbourhood or city.

But though there is little unity or consistency among these various organizations, there are a number of common features. They promote community and work toward the strengthening of local neighbourhoods. Community groups operate within a political sphere. They work hard to shape the opinions of the public about their issue, either through the media or through their own publications. And ultimately their goal is to get a favourable political decision on the issue or issues that they see as important.

Anyone who has been involved in community groups knows that this is time-consuming work, filled with frustrations, disappointments, and few victories, and yet people are increasingly getting involved. Many find it inherently rewarding because it is an immediate way to contribute to their community and enhance the lives of their neighbours.

The best way, perhaps the only way, to understand community groups is to look at different organizations and understand the issues that they have fought, their histories, successes, and failures. But first, a little background.

* * *

A NOTE ON HISTORY AND STRATEGY

There have been grassroots community groups in Western societies at least as far back as the peasant revolts that swept Europe in the fourteenth century. Those revolts are interesting because they started as reasonable demands, but the autocratic governments of the day suppressed the peasants with military force, believing they were fomenting revolution. Citizen movements can only flourish in democracies that tolerate dissent and opposition.[2]

In Canada there have been many protest movements. We have seen some of them in the histories of the trade union and the environmental movement. As early as 1900 in Toronto, ratepayer groups had sprung up in some of the more affluent neighbourhoods, but it was only after the Second World War that a number of groups began to emerge and play a political role in the city.

For example, in the late 1950s the Annex Ratepayers' Association participated in the creation of the city's official plan.[3] That group continues to operate today.

As groups emerged there were attacks on them. "Who do these people represent?" was a common complaint of municipal politicians. "They don't hold elected office."[4] The old idea was that only the elected politician, who had a mandate from the people, had the right to voice opinions and make decisions on issues. That is the view of representative democracy. Today the operating principle is that all citizens have the right to participate in politics, but only elected politicians have the right to vote on issues in municipal councils or parliaments.

The one political activist who tried to develop community activism into a political tactic for change was the organizer Saul Alinsky. He worked mainly with poor people, often African Americans, in large U.S. cities, but his ideas and tactics have been adapted by different organizations.

His approach has been called "creative confrontation," and among organizers today it still holds an almost romantic attraction. These are some ideas that he outlined in his book *Rules for Radicals*. "Power is not what you have, but what the enemy thinks you have." "Make the enemy live up to its own rules." "Ridicule is man's most potent weapon." "Keep the pressure on. Never give up." "The threat is more terrifying than the thing itself."[5]

Alinsky used confrontation to influence events, often by frightening the opposition into making concessions. By the end of the 1960s his influence was very broad among organizers, particularly those working with groups of poor people. Hilary Rodham Clinton wrote a master's thesis on his work, and Barack Obama used his tactics when he was an organizer in Chicago as a young man.

In Canada, some Alinsky-styled groups were founded in the late 1960s and early 1970s, but his approach was never widely adopted. Confrontational politics is only successful if the people in the group feel abused, disenfranchised, or angry. That is why the organizers who adopted Alinsky tactics worked with poor people.[6] I worked as an organizer with a welfare rights organization in Hamilton in the early 1970s. At first the group won major concessions using confrontation, but as time wore on we became a grassroots advocacy group defending the rights of individuals.[7]

In Canada those who became involved in urban politics were a broad mix of classes and ethnic groups, not just poor people. Although they protested decisions, groups like this accepted the legitimacy of the existing political process and the right of elected politicians to make the final decision. Community activists in Canada are, almost without exception, reformers not radicals. In fact, most participants in community groups tend to be middle-class, older people who are well integrated into their community and are comfortable participating within the political system.

It was the issues that created this citizen's movement. At the end of the 1960s and early 1970s disruptive changes came to Canadian cities and affected those living in established inner-city neighbourhoods. These were invasive developments of either high-rise projects that destroyed houses, or public projects like highways, street widening, or urban renewal. They sparked urban protest movements in Toronto, Montreal, and Vancouver that led to political change.

At the same time, a new set of ideas about cities and how they functioned emerged. Jane Jacob's book *The Death and Life of Great American Cities* was the most influential, but there were other important voices who contributed to this debate. Their ideas emphasized the importance of neighbourhoods and street life. They were critical of large megaprojects, invasive traffic, and the intellectual arrogance of planners who wanted to impose developments in the name of "progress."

It was this combination of new ideas and the threat of disruptive changes to neighbourhoods that, in time, transformed the way planning was done and how urban politics was practised in Canada. It is worth looking at the issues and events that led to this transformation in each of the three largest cities because it tells us much about the way grassroots democratic politics is practised today.

* * *

TORONTO

It was the combination of different issues — issues like urban renewal, high-rises imposed on established neighbourhoods, and expressways — that mobilized citizens and led to the transformation of Toronto municipal politics.

Trefann Court, a low-income neighbourhood, became a leading edge of the new politics more by circumstance than design. It is a small community a little east of the downtown, north of Queen Street and east of Parliament to River Street. The neighbourhood was a mix of industry and working-class housing where about fifteen hundred people lived. In the 1950s a proposal was made to demolish the area and convert it into high-rise public housing. In 1966 the city moved to expropriate the houses using the urban renewal program, in which the costs would be shared by the federal, provincial, and municipal governments.

The residents were very uneasy about the proposal. Close by was Regent Park, a public housing project developed in the 1940s, which was fast becoming a troubled neighbourhood. St. James Town, a high-rise, high-density community of twenty thousand low-income residents was within walking distance. People were concerned about being displaced from their homes, but they also worried that expropriation would lead to low values for their property.

Community organizers began working in the area. One of them, John Sewell, would later become a progressive city councillor and mayor of Toronto. As citizens became involved and organizers began to probe the workings of city hall, secret plans were revealed. One of them was a plan to tear down a large block of houses in nearby Cabbagetown to create a retail mall and parking lot. City hall politicians and bureaucrats had little interest in what the local people had to say. There were angry meetings between community members, city staff, and politicians. The media began to take interest, particularly reporters from the *Globe and Mail*. Academics began to write about the growing resistance to city plans that would destroy neighbourhoods.

As the issue intensified, the residents became increasingly sophisticated in their dealing with these complex issues. Initially many only wanted better value for their homes, but as time went on their demands included stopping the demolitions and ending the entire urban renewal program. They wanted a new plan that would save and improve the community, not destroy it.

In the end they got what they wanted, but not without hard work and an endless number of meetings. In 1969 the city abandoned its plan of demolishing the community, and in that same year John Sewell was elected onto Toronto City Council. Trefann Count is now a mixed-use community with subsidized and market housing. In the process the federal government cancelled the urban renewal program, and the people of Trefann Court played a major role in transforming Toronto's planning process.

There were other serious problems with development and developers. Large office buildings in Toronto's Financial District were being built and some beautiful old office buildings with unique features were demolished. Few people lived in the downtown, but the destruction stirred the interest of people who advocated the preservation of the city's architectural heritage.

In the late 1960s and early 1970s the number of neighbourhoods threatened by demolition and high-rise construction grew. After the opening of the Bloor-Danforth subway the area immediately north of High Park was bought up by developers. This was a prosperous middle-class neighbourhood with classic Edwardian houses. The developers wanted all of the buildings, but some homeowners resisted. Block-busting tactics were used by moving biker gangs into empty houses with the sole purpose of disturbing the peace and driving out the remaining residents. In the end the developers won these battles, but not before raucous Toronto council debates and media attention.

There were other serious issues involving developers, threats of demolitions in established neighbourhoods, and high-rises. These included West St. James Town, Lionstar at Bloor and Dufferin Streets, and Windless, west of University Avenue. An especially nasty battle erupted between the residents on Marlborough Avenue and the Marathon Realty Company.

Whenever issues like these were debated at Toronto City Hall, the citizen's gallery filled, deputations were made, and the press covered the issues in detail. Demands were made to protect neighbourhoods, not demolish them. The public was stirred. Community groups were proliferating across the city. Some were set up specifically to fight development. Others were ratepayer groups designed to monitor what was going on and bring any threat to the attention of the public. The Confederation of Residents and Ratepayer Associations (CORRA) was a coalition of community groups founded to deal with city-wide issues and to share information.

The other major issue that had a huge impact on Toronto city politics in the late 1960s and early 1970s was the Stop Spadina movement. Much has been written about Stop Spadina, and it is still worth remembering the importance of this struggle. It literally saved the downtown and inner-city neighbourhoods from the decay that is so widespread in American cities.

In the late 1950s and 1960s the belief was that cars not only would be the dominant mode of transportation, but the only efficient way to move around cities. In Toronto plans were made for six interconnected inner-city expressways. The Spadina Expressway would run from Highway 401 south through several neighbourhoods and connect with the Gardiner near the Waterfront. It would destroy thousands of homes, divide neighbourhoods, and make the city car-dependent.

As construction began in 1967 the opposition to the expressway intensified. Led by residents who lived in the path of the highway, it was the community groups who led the fight. Thousands of citizens became involved, including Jane Jacobs, who had moved to Toronto before this fight erupted. The controversy, and all of the attention surrounding it, helped people in the city to understand how important this issue was in the struggle to keep the city livable.

Finally, Ontario premier Bill Davis cancelled the project on June 3, 1971. When he made the announcement in the legislature, he said, in part, "If we are building a transportation system to serve the automobile, the Spadina Expressway would be a good place to start. But if we are building a transportation system to serve the people, the Spadina Expressway would be a good place to stop."

Through this turbulent time of the late 1960s and early 1970s, the Toronto city council was polarized. On one side was the so-called Old Guard, which supported the old way of doing things, including the destruction of neighbourhoods and building more high-rises and expressways. The Old Guard believed that citizens should basically shut up and let elected representatives decide what was best. On the other side was the Reform Group, which advocated citizen involvement, neighbourhood control of the planning process, and the end of megaprojects. In the 1972 municipal election David Crombie was elected mayor and the reform slate made up the majority of council.

That election marks the beginning of a more participatory and democratic style of politics in Toronto. Other large Canadian cities went through a similar, but different process.

* * *

MONTREAL

Milton Parc in Montreal was one of the most dramatic of the new urban struggles that polarized neighbourhoods and cities in this country.

The Milton Parc neighbourhood is close to Montreal's downtown commercial district and a short walk to McGill University. The streets are lined with elegant Victorian Greystone buildings that have provided housing for more than one hundred years.[8]

The first occupants of Milton Parc were wealthy families, but by the 1930s almost all of them had moved out. Houses were subdivided into spacious apartments that provided good housing with low rents. The residents were made up of French, English, and immigrant families. There were a number of McGill University students and some professors. Parts of the buildings in this lively mix were occupied by small shops, bookstores, bars, and restaurants.

During the 1950s and 1960s a building boom came to downtown Montreal. Because Milton Parc was close to the downtown, land values began to rise and speculators were active. Some buildings were demolished and replaced by apartment buildings that charged higher rents.

It was during this time that Concordia Estates, a Montreal development company, acquired a six-block parcel in Milton Parc neighbourhood. Plans were made for La Cité Concordia. Phase 1 included three twenty-five-storey apartment buildings, a five-hundred-room hotel, and a twenty-nine storey office building. Phase 2 of the project — seven hundred apartment units — would come later. In the summer of 1972 Concordia demolished and cleared the property along Parc Avenue for Phase 1.

It was then that local citizens became involved. People in the remaining part of Milton Parc organized. Their objective was to stop the development plans of Concordia and save what was left of the community. Various tactics were employed. Residents held a sit-in at the Concordia offices. This led to arrests and media attention. There were public meetings where the plans of the developer were criticized and denounced. Both the French and English media were urged to report on the issue, and over time Montreal journalists followed the story in detail.

In the meantime, Concordia drifted into financial difficulties. Phase 1 was completed in 1976, but the company's other projects were not as successful as predicted. More than once, construction for Phase 2 was announced and then cancelled because the developer could not arrange financing. Soon it became public knowledge that the company was trying to sell the Phase 2 property. All of this worked to the advantage of the residents.

Various influential people began to support the Milton Parc residents. Some were progressive planners and other professionals who questioned the value of Concordia's plans. The most important was architect Phyllis Lambert, both an advocate for the protection of architectural heritage and a member of the wealthy Bronfman family, who were prominent Liberals.

On May 16, 1979, just days before a federal election, CMHC (the federal housing agency) announced that it would buy the Phase 2 property for $5.5 million, renovate the houses, and turn them into housing co-operatives.[9] This was a complete victory for the residents, but it also helped to bail out Concordia by providing them with much-needed cash.

Today what is left of the buildings in the Milton Parc neighbourhood has been restored and renovated. There are six hundred units organized into twenty-three co-ops and non-profits. Rents remain affordable, and the residents continue to maintain all of the property. It remains a mixed income community with French, English, and immigrant families.

Milton Parc was an important community issue in Montreal because it illustrated the problem of development, but there were others. One event that galvanized community activists and architectural preservationists was the demolition of the Van Horne mansion.

This was a classic Greystone house on Sherbrooke Street in Montreal's fabled Golden Square Mile. The mansion was built in 1869 for John Hamilton, the president of the Merchants' Bank of Canada. It was purchased in 1889 by William Van Horne, the president of the Canadian Pacific Railway when the railway was built across the continent to British Columbia. Van Horne was the most prominent Canadian businessman of his day.

In 1973 the developer David Azrieli applied to demolish the mansion and replace it with a seventeen-storey building. There were protests and a campaign to save the mansion, but in the end it was demolished. Mayor Jean Drapeau justified the demolition by saying that the building could not be saved for cultural reasons because its history was Anglo Canadian, not French Canadian. That only infuriated the opponents and heightened the controversy.

The incident played an important role in Montreal politics. This is the description of one commentator: "It was a moment that marked the city's transition to a modern metropolis, and it changed the way people thought about their past and their future."[10]

The Montreal Citizens' Movement (MCM), a municipal political party, was founded in the same year as the demolition. This was a left of centre coalition of French and English political activists. Jean Drapeau remained popular, particularly with the French-speaking population, but after he retired in 1986 the MCM defeated Drapeau's Civic Action Party and took power in the City of Montreal under the leadership of Jean Doré.

* * *

VANCOUVER

Prior to the 1970s Vancouver had a political system designed to take politics out of municipal government. It was called the "non-partisan tradition," but in fact it brought thirty-five years of business domination to city hall. There were no political parties, and no ward system. Councillors were elected at large, across the whole city. That meant most of those who were elected came from the wealthier West End of the city. The administration was led by an executive committee made up of two councillors. But, in fact, the real power was held by senior administrators who were to make decisions on technical grounds.[11] All of this led to elitist, hierarchical, and conservative city government that paid little attention to citizens.

After the Second World War, Vancouverites, like people in the rest of North America, bought cars in increasing numbers, and like in other cities, Vancouver administrators began to plan a series of expressways, or freeways, as they were locally called, to accommodate the rapidly increasing number of cars.

In 1959 the "Freeway with Rapid Transit" report was published by the city. It had little to do with rapid transit; the report was a freeway plan for Vancouver and the broader metropolitan region. It called for four freeways that were to converge on the Burrard Peninsula, the central business district of the city. There were different configurations depending on densities, but in the main commercial area of Vancouver, the freeway was a sub-grade ditch two-hundred feet wide, with eight lanes and thirty-foot-high walls. All of the freeways called for the wholesale destruction of neighbourhoods, particularly poor communities, creating impassable barriers and small, isolated pockets of houses. This report was to become the master plan for Vancouver freeways for the next ten years.

But unlike in other North American cities where powerful politicians and civic administrators pushed expressways through the central core of cities, there were major political problems in Vancouver. The broader metropolitan region was divided into several independent municipalities, but there was no metro-area political body that could take responsibility for the planning and implementation of the freeway network. (This was the case in Toronto.) Vancouver was the central core, and its administration did most of the planning, but the other municipalities had to be consulted, and they had to find funds in their limited budgets.

The provincial Social Credit government at the time had little interest in Vancouver. Their political support came from the B.C. Interior, and the province was busy building a highway system to connect centres in the Interior. The province provided little to no help in drawing the scattered Vancouver-area municipalities together to plan and execute the freeway plan. More important, they initially provided no financial aid. Later, when they did promise funding, the terms kept changing. All this led to what one observer called an ad-hoc planning system that kept changing as different decisions were made.[12]

The result of these political problems and uncertainties was delay. Nothing seemed to happen, and yet the freeway issue was constantly in the news. Citizens became aware that something drastic was going on in their city, and that left many very uneasy. By the middle of the 1960s there were growing concerns across North America about the negative impact of expressways on urban areas. Protest movements emerged in New York, Boston, Toronto, San Francisco, and other cities.

It was 1967 that the freeway debate dramatically emerged in Vancouver. Concerns were initially expressed by Chinese businessmen who objected that the most important freeway was to cut off a portion of Chinatown, a major tourist attraction and thriving business district. Soon a number of academics, almost all of them planners and social scientists, mounted a major critique of the plan, pointing out the scores of deficiencies and the huge problems that the expressways would bring to the city.

On November 23, 1967, a meeting called to discuss the freeway issue was attended by hundreds of citizens. It exploded into "the wildest, stormy meeting ever seen at city hall."[13] The next day Mayor Tom Campbell attacked the opposition. He described the meeting as a "near riot," ignoring the fact that it was his political maneuverings that had made the people angry in the first place. His statements only inflamed the situation.

As the meetings went on over the coming months and years, the number of people opposed to the freeway plan grew. Every meeting was packed with opponents. Deficiencies in the plan pointed out by the public were legion. The most telling one was that the plan looked only at projected traffic, not the impact of traffic on communities. Even the traffic estimates were more than ten years old. Some of the strongest attacks came from citizens who were angry about the secretive nature of the Vancouver planning system.

The core opposition came from people who lived in the inner city neighbourhoods, but as the issue dragged on many others joined with them. Business groups in the central part of the city initially supported the freeway plan, but in time they came to see that the expressway would harm the downtown, and they became opponents. It took time, but even some conservative city councillors abandoned the plan because they could see that they would lose the next election if they continued their support.

It was not until 1972, with the election of Art Phillips as mayor, along with councillors from TEAM, a municipal political party he founded, that the freeway plan was finally put to rest. Vancouver today is one of the few North American cities that does not have freeways in its downtown and inner suburbs. But the freeway debate did much more than cancel a group of highways. It transformed Vancouver city politics. The redevelopment of False Creek and Granville Island was started. Local neighbourhood planning was emphasized.

Today planning decisions are largely independent of council influence in Vancouver. The city does not allow road widening. Single-occupancy vehicles are discouraged, and priority is given first to pedestrians, then cyclists, then transit, and finally to private vehicles. There are high densities in the downtown. Four- or five-storey-high podiums of buildings come out to the sidewalk. They are usually occupied by offices or retail businesses. Tall, narrow towers of apartments or condominiums sprout out of the centre of the podiums. There are ample parks and walkways along the waterfront. All this gives the city a human scale, despite the high densities. This approach to planning has come to be called the Vancouver Model.

To say the freeway debates of the 1960s and 1970s were the sole reason for the current livability of Vancouver is an exaggeration, but the engagement in public life of Vancouverites is part of the legacy. That tradition was forged in the freeway debate.

* * *

THE URBAN POLITICAL TRANSFORMATION

Even though these three cities — Toronto, Montreal, and Vancouver — are separated by geography, culture, and political systems, there is a remarkable similarity in their political histories from the 1960s to the 1980s. This is no accident. Each city was going through similar changes at about the same time and each developed similar solutions.

Established neighbourhoods were experiencing redevelopment pressures from private developers who wanted to build high-rise projects. Government programs like urban renewal brought additional problems. Expressways played a particularly important role in both Toronto and Vancouver. Montreal built expressways in the same period, but power was centralized in the popular mayor Jean Drapeau, and he easily defeated the opposition.

The issue of invasive development in established neighbourhoods has been largely solved. Even developers have learned that this will only lead to trouble. Traffic remains the major problem for our cities. There will be no more expressways built, but traffic clogs the streets and highways despite increased public investments in transit.

Before this period of transition the three cities were governed by top-down politicians or administrators who used their power to impose their policies and projects with little consultation. The issues that emerged in the late 1960s and 1970s were catalysts that led to major political changes. Those changes came at almost identical times in Vancouver and Toronto. In Montreal it took longer, because Jean Drapeau was entrenched, but after the election of the MCM, the reforms were very similar to the other cities'.

At the core of the political issues in all three cities was the demand for greater citizen participation and more open, transparent government. The result in every case was greater grassroots democracy and public participation in the planning process.

This movement affected smaller cities to a lesser effect. Hamilton and Ottawa have had reform movements, but they were less successful. Calgary, Edmonton, and Winnipeg have had reform mayors who have brought changes to the way that government is practised. In all of these cities there is now far greater opportunity for participation in local governments.

* * *

CITIZEN PARTICIPATION

It was these series of events in cities during the 1960s and 1970s that encouraged the growth of community groups. Since that time the number of people and groups participating has grown enormously. Today citizens expressing their views on issues are accepted as a normal part of politics. Many progressive politicians even encourage citizens to form groups and make their views known. This has helped to transform our political life and make it more participatory and democratic.

The number of groups active in Canada today is far too numerous to describe or even summarize. This is a small sampling of a few groups. I apologize for the Toronto-centric nature of the sample, but I wanted to include groups that I have some first-hand knowledge about. The examples range from a small neighbourhood association to large city-wide groups that have had a major impact.

* * *

CHURCH AND WELLESLEY NEIGHBOURHOOD ASSOCIATION

In 2010 a few residents of the Church and Wellesley area in downtown Toronto were alarmed about what residents felt was an inappropriate development in their neighbourhood. They successfully opposed this development with the help of their local city councillor. As they explain on their website, "In rallying together, the community felt the power of our collective action for the first time."[14]

Out of that successful action the Church and Wellesley Neighbourhood Association was formed. It has become an organization that monitors the many new developments that have been proposed, or are under development in the neighbourhood. The aim of the group is to protect the unique architectural heritage of the community, and advocate for the adoption of innovative and inclusive city building practices. Members are not opposed to development; they want to ensure that it meets the needs and character of the community. They also lobby to improve parks and make the streets safer and more beautiful.

Communication about new development in the community is a very important part of the group's activities. They provide information to residents via their newsletter, and make an effort to communicate the views of their association to various individuals and public groups, from the city councillor to city staff, the police, and the local business association. This work is done entirely on a voluntary basis.

There are dozens of organizations like this across Toronto.

* * *

RED HILL CREEK EXPRESSWAY

The Red Hill Creek Expressway in Hamilton was a proposal to build a four-lane highway from the Queen Elizabeth Expressway to the Lincoln Alexander Parkway on the Mountain. It was to go through the Red Hill Creek Valley and punch through the crest of the Niagara Escarpment. In the 1980s the project was finally approved. Shortly after, a citizen's group called Save our Valley was formed to oppose it. They advocated that the road be cancelled and that the Red Hill Creek Valley should become a park.

Before construction could begin the Ontario NDP government was elected in 1990, and they cancelled the project. But demands that the highway be constructed continued both from residents of East Mountain (who would benefit from the road) and from the majority of the members of

Hamilton City Council. To try and resolve the dispute, the NDP government appointed David Crombie, the former mayor of Toronto and federal cabinet minister, to try and work out a compromise. He proposed making it a smaller highway. That satisfied no one and the controversy continued.

In 1995 the new Conservative provincial government of Mike Harris reinstated the funding. The Liberal federal government, however, delayed the project yet again by ordering that a full environmental assessment of the highway be conducted.

By 2003 the environmental assessment was completed. Hamilton had elected a new mayor and the highway project was approved again by the city. As construction prepared to get underway, opposition began in earnest. A group called Friends of Red Hill Valley was formed. The members of the Six Nations Reserve became involved. Access roads were blocked. Injunctions were filed. The police cleared the roads. Young people climbed trees slated to be cut down and refused to come down. Despite all of the protests, in 2004 construction began and the highway was finished in 2007.

The long struggle against the Red Hill Expressway politicized a number of people in Hamilton. Active environmental and protest groups emerged in the city, but they have been unable to gain a majority on council.

* * *

CITIZENS FOR CLEAN AIR

No citizen's group has had such political impact on Ontario provincial politics as Citizens for Clean Air. The actions of the group led to the cancellation of two gas-fired power plants, the resignation of Energy Minister Chris Bentley, and contributed to the resignation of Premier Dalton McGuinty.

After the election of the McGuinty government in 2003, they established the policy of closing all of the coal-fired power plants in the province. Then in 2008, the government decided that two gas-powered plants were needed to service the growing GTA. It was announced that one would be built in Mississauga and the other in Oakville. It did not take long before residents began to organize against the plants. They called themselves Citizens for Clean Air.

Various events and protests were mounted and the provincial government responded by cancelling the Oakville plant in October 2010, but they insisted that the Mississauga plant was essential for meeting the power needs of the growing GTA.

A provincial election was called in September 2011, and the Liberals were in trouble. They needed to win the seats in the vote-rich GTA suburbs if they were to stay in power. Citizens for Clean Air stepped up their campaign for the closure of the Mississauga plant, and as the election progressed it became a big issue in key ridings. The pressure was so great that a week before the election McGuinty cancelled the Mississauga plant.

This was enough for the Liberals to win a minority government, but it was not the end of the issue. The members of the citizens' group were satisfied because they got what they wanted, but the opposition was on the attack over the cancellation of the power plants. Later it was revealed that the Ontario government would have to pay $930 million in cancellation penalties to the contractors. Another element of the scandal was when it was learned that the premier's staff had also deleted relevant emails about the issue. The opposition claimed this was part of a cover-up.

In resigning the premier was accepting responsibility for the affair. Clearly McGuinty's handling of the issue tarnished his image.

* * *

COMMUNITYAIR AND NOJETSTO

The struggle to close the Island Airport (known now as the Billy Bishop Toronto City Airport) has been one of the longest, most intense community struggles in Toronto's history. It began back in the 1930s when it was first proposed that the city build two airports: one on Toronto Island and the other near the small town of Malton, just outside the city.[15] (Malton soon became the city's major airport. Today it is known as Pearson International Airport, and it is by far the largest in the country.)

The city councillors' vehement objections to building the Island Airport back in the 1930s would be familiar to us today. The airport was to be in the centre of the city's greatest recreational resource — Toronto Island park —

the harbour, and Lake Ontario. But despite the opposition, a slim majority of council members voted to build the airport.

Shortly after Island Airport was completed, the Second World War broke out and it was used as a training facility for airmen. Even then, the noise from the aircraft was so great that the authorities decided the training facility needed to be decamped to Muskoka. After the war, traffic at the airport was light. A flying school and private planes used the airport. Several commercial airlines were announced but all ultimately failed.

In the 1980s Air Otonabee (later City Express) began to operate short-haul flights using the Island Airport as its hub. The city, the Toronto Harbour Commission, and Transport Canada entered into the Tripartite Agreement to govern the operations of the airport. The planes were to be short takeoff and landing (STOL), no jets, and no fixed link from the Island to the mainland. But still City Express ultimately failed.

Communities close to the airport were growing as Toronto's Waterfront was undergoing redevelopment. One of the first neighbourhoods to complete construction was Bathurst Quay, which is adjacent to the airport. Some buildings are less than half a kilometre from the main airport runway.

Increasing numbers of residents were complaining about the airport. It was losing money and there was a strong lobby to close it and turn the airport lands to other uses. Then in the 1990s the federal government created new legislation called the Canada Marine Act. After that, the Toronto Port Authority, the successor of the Toronto Harbour Commission, began to aggressively market the airport. They found Robert Deluce, an airline entrepreneur, who said he would like to establish an airline using turboprop aircraft.

In 2002 the Port Authority proposed building a bridge to the airport to facilitate the expansion of the airport and support Deluce's proposal to establish a short-haul commercial airline. This became a major political issue in the 2003 municipal election. By that time, a citizens-based activist group called CommunityAIR had been formed, and it played a role in the election by opposing the bridge. David Miller, the only major candidate who opposed the bridge, was elected mayor, and it seemed like the whole airport proposal was finally on its last legs. But it didn't work out that way.

In 2006 Porter Airlines was founded with Robert Deluce as president and CEO. The airline began flying Q400 turboprop planes out of the Island. The Q400 is not a STOL but the Port Authority found a way to allow its use at the Island. Later, the Port Authority even built a pedestrian tunnel (another violation of the Tripartite Agreement) but they refused to call it a fixed link and claimed it was legal. Community protests grew louder and more strident but the Port Authority simply ignored the controversy.

In 2013 Robert Deluce announced that he wanted permission to fly jets out of the Island. That led to the creation of yet another community group, NoJetsTO, who mounted a major public campaign against the use of the Island Airport for jets. In 2015 shortly after the federal election, the new Trudeau government announced that they would not allow jets. This time, at least, the Port Authority was forced to follow the terms of the Tripartite Agreement.

An uneasy calm has settled in. Community groups along Toronto's Waterfront are opposed to the Island Airport, but Porter and the Toronto Port Authority still have considerable influence. It remains to be seen how the issue will be resolved.

* * *

WATERFRONT TORONTO

Waterfront Toronto is not a community group at all. It is a public agency established in 2001 and funded by the federal, provincial, and Toronto governments. Its mandate is to plan and redevelop the industrial lands that spread along the Waterfront from Dowling Avenue in the west to Coxwell Avenue in the east, in total about two thousand acres of land. This is the largest redevelopment project in North America.

When the planners first gathered to work on the project they faced a problem. They were trained in a new type of planning process that engaged ordinary citizens as advisors. Those participating in the planning process are usually the clients who are paying for the building. Others are local residents who will be affected by the building. The problem with the Waterfront Toronto project was that there were no residents. This was empty land that had once had industry. There were architects, developers, builders, and several politicians involved in the project, but no ordinary citizens or future residents. What were the planners to do?

In fact, the solution was quite simple. They asked for volunteers who would donate their time to examine the plans in detail. Their role was to critique the plans as if they were residents. Once the call went out they found many ordinary people willing to become involved.

Planning this massive project has been a long and complicated process that is still ongoing. Volunteers spent hours looking at the plans and discussing them in detail, and the professional staff who worked on the project say that the comments from the volunteers were invaluable.

Plans were changed as the ideas flowed, sometimes changed fundamentally, and gradually in the process, the plans were improved and refined. Buildings were redesigned and public spaces altered to make them more functional and attractive. Those involved in the process, both citizens and experts, say that it was richly rewarding on a personal level. Citizens performed a valuable public service in helping the experts to refine and improve the plans.

*   *   *

PARTICIPATION AND PUBLIC PLANNING

There is an important message in this that we should take to heart. We should be designing our cities for the people who live in them — not for the politicians or bureaucrats, not for the planners and architects, not for the storeowners or the business community, and not for those who drive cars — but for the people who will be using the buildings and the public spaces.

Top-down planning has been a disaster for our cities. It has resulted in expressways destroying communities, cars dominating the streets and making them unsafe and the public domain unpleasant. Participation is the only way that we can recapture the human dimension of our cities.

It was the citizens of Vancouver who understood that freeways would destroy their city. Fortunately, they had the political savvy to rescue the planning process from the traffic engineers and freeway advocates, just as the residents of Milton Parc in Montreal rescued their magnificent Greystones from the wrecking ball.

The same is true of other groups that we have described. Workers and their unions helped to transform factories and offices into places where they could grow and prosper. Co-ops and non-profits tell the same story. It was by working together in a co-operative way that people solved their economic problems. Environmental groups have been far ahead of the rest of us in seeing the problems of our consumer society. If only we had had the sense to listen to them rather than the powerful business interests, we could have avoided the crisis of climate change and other environmental problems.

It is democratic participation that is the key ingredient in all of these movements. Citizen environmentalists, not government, were the ones who recognized the dangers of pollution. Workers fought for more humanitarian workplaces and a living wage. And it is citizens who know how to develop livable communities. The benefit of participatory democracy is not only the involvement of citizens in the democratic process; it also leads to better decisions because those involved have a deep and comprehensive understanding of the issues.

But before we leave this discussion of grassroots democratic organizations, let's look at groups that would benefit enormously if they could become more effective advocates.

CHAPTER 10

THE EXCLUDED

Until now we have been discussing established groups whose voices are heard in the political arena. Trade unions, co-ops, non-profits, environmental groups, and community associations all participate openly in public life. These are the strongest grassroots organizations in the country and the pioneers of the participatory democracy that is emerging in Canada.

There are, however, even more people who have no group to speak on their behalf. Many suffer from a history of prejudice and deprivation that has left them powerless, frustrated, and angry. If we are to build a more democratic country, it is these people who must be included. Their voices must be heard.

These are examples of groups that are excluded and live on the margins.

* * *

ABORIGINAL PEOPLES

Aboriginal is the inclusive term used to describe First Nations, Métis, and Inuit. Not all, but many of the people in this group suffer from poverty, discrimination, and a type of cultural crisis that has left them disoriented, and even rootless.

This is the result of a history that left aboriginal peoples without their land, and unable to carry on with their traditional way of life. Many First Nations people were settled on isolated reserves, often cut off from other people of their own cultural groups. The effort of the Canadian government to assimilate them through residential schools was so ineffective that it compounded the problems and led to serious issues of abuse.

All this has resulted in the poverty of a large number of First Nations. They suffer from high levels of unemployment, substandard living conditions and overcrowding on many reservations, high rates of preventable health problems, elevated suicide rates among young people, and high levels of incarceration. Thousands of First Nations children are in the care of provincial child-welfare authorities. There are boil-water advisories on more than seventy-five reserves that are home to 152,000 people.[1]

Aboriginal people are the responsibility of the federal government. Depending on the government in power, this responsibility has been either ignored or dealt with in legalistic ways. Over the decades there have been twenty major changes to the Indian Act. In 1991 the Royal Commission on Aboriginal People was established and came up with a list of 440 recommendations. Many were acted on, but none of the changes have resulted in any significant improvement in living conditions for aboriginal peoples. In fact, only rarely has there been a serious effort to solve the social problems faced by aboriginal people and that is the crucial issue today.

Education is a good example of the neglect. The federal government spending on education on reserves is between 20 and 50 percent lower than provincial educational funding. In 2011 the high school graduation rate for First Nations students living on reserves was 35.8 percent, compared with 78 percent for the population as a whole.[2]

In 2005 Prime Minister Paul Martin's government negotiated an agreement that came to be called the Kelowna Accord, named after the city where it was signed. The agreement was accepted by the Assembly of First Nations, the federal government, the provinces, and the territories. The Liberals had a minority government at the time, and Jack Layton, leader of the NDP, supported the agreement so it would pass in the House of Commons. The accord was to provide over $5 billion in spending over five years to improve education, employment opportunities, and living conditions on reserves.

Before the Kelowna Accord could be ratified by Parliament, however, an election was called and Stephen Harper's Conservatives were elected with a minority government. They refused to support the accord and it died. For the next ten years of Conservative government very little was done to help aboriginals. The Justin Trudeau Liberal government has promised more support for programs to help aboriginal communities, but as of this writing nothing concrete has been announced. For decades very little has been done to improve the living conditions of any of the aboriginal people.

Increased public funding is essential, but the only way that will happen is by public pressure, and that must come from aboriginal people themselves. This has been happening. The Assembly of First Nations has a history going back to 1968. They have been playing a very active role in negotiating with government and keeping issues before the public. Some concessions have been made, but the living conditions on reserves have changed very little.

In frustration, some First Nations groups have become more outspoken. Many have resorted to acts of civil disobedience. Road blocks have been set up and trains have been stopped by protesters. Recently scores of aboriginals in British Columbia opposed the Northern Gateway oil pipeline, which they claim will harm the environment and be of no benefit to their people. The Trudeau government has killed this pipeline, largely because of the opposition of First Nations bands.

In December 2012 four women — three First Nations and one non-Aboriginal ally — founded a group called Idle No More, rooted, they say, in "indigenous ways of knowing." This is a militant organization made up primarily of young First Nations, as well as other supporters who agree with their goals and approach. They have shifted away from a focus on living conditions to talk about pipelines, resource exploitation, environmental sustainability, and human rights. They say they want nation-to-nation negotiations on these issues. To date there have been more than one hundred Idle No More protests.

The polarization has become more intense in recent years. On a number of occasions frustration has led to anger and confrontations. First Nations people are beginning to mobilize to force improvements in their living standards from the federal government. Many Canadians are alarmed at this, but it should be seen as a healthy sign. They are gathering strength and confidence by participating in the political process because that is the only way that they can achieve resolution of their grievances and the ability to improve living standards.

They know that only protest and participation will create the political conditions that will lead to change, and they are not about to give up the struggle until they get them.

* * *

THE POOR

The largest group with no political voice in Canada is the poor. People are concerned about poverty in this country. The mountains of reports that lie dormant on library shelves gathering dust are testament to that, but they will remain there until a movement is built that demands change.

Despite all of the attention given to poverty, Canadian governments and agencies cannot even agree on who is poor and who is not. In recent years, the federal government has refused to endorse any measure of poverty by establishing a poverty line. The last attempt in 2005 put the poverty rate in Canada at 10.8 percent. A recent study in Hamilton put the poverty rate in that city at 18.1 percent. The conservative Fraser Institute put the poverty level in the country at 4.9 percent in 2004, and the Toronto Regional Board of Trade estimated 10.7 percent lived in poverty in the Toronto area.[3]

But despite the politics, these are some of the important things we know about the issue. Poverty rates vary as the business cycle changes. The poor include people on social assistance, as well as the working poor. More women than men live in poverty because women more often have custody of children when there is marriage breakdown. Housing costs are a major determinant. Large cities like Vancouver, Toronto, Calgary, and Ottawa have much higher rents than smaller centres. Children live in poverty at a higher rate than adults. The Hamilton study found 18.1 percent of the city's population lived in poverty, while the rate for children was 25 percent. Similar results have been found across the country. The poor have higher health risks, poorer nutrition, lower life expectancy, poorer quality of life, higher rates of addiction, and higher crime rates. One study found that poverty in Canada today is worse than in 1989.

To illustrate the political nature of poverty in this country, until the 1960s seniors had the highest rates of poverty of any group in the country. But a high proportion of seniors vote in elections — a much higher proportion than do young people, as we will see. Politicians decided something had to be done because of the political pressure they were receiving. The problem was solved with the increase in Old Age Security, the Canada Pension Plan, and income supplement programs for seniors. There has also been significant public funding for affordable housing and long-term care for seniors. Today poverty among seniors has decreased significantly.

The question is, why don't we eliminate all poverty? It is not because of a lack of funds. There is a small group of the very poor who will be difficult to help because they need special programs. These include the homeless, those with addictions, and the mentally ill. But for others, the problem can be dealt with primarily by boosting incomes. Some argue that if we increase incomes for that group it will reduce other costs like health care and the expense of taking children into care.

One reason we do so little is because of our values. We believe people should solve their own problems. We say, "When the going gets tough, the tough get going." There is a fear that if welfare rates are too high people will give up working. We give all sorts of aid to businesses, but other than a poverty level of support, the poor are on their own. Not even the leaders of the women's movement have stepped forward to decry the high levels of poverty among women. We blame the poor for their poverty and that gives us an excuse for doing nothing.

But there is another reason. The poor have been unable to mobilize into a political movement to participate in the political system and demand that their problems be taken seriously. That was not always the case. The Depression inspired a growing movement demanding that poverty be eliminated. Protests happened in every city, and governments grew alarmed.

Today there is no movement of poor people and virtually no individual willing to talk about the problems that they face. Social workers and health care workers speak out about it, but not the people who live in poverty every day. The only explanation for why they are unable to speak out is shame. They blame themselves for their poverty, and remain silent. Nothing is done because there is no political demand for change.[4]

The only thing that will bring change is empowerment: speaking out, participating, demanding change.

* * *

MINORITY GROUPS

Today Canada is ranked as one of the most tolerant countries in the world.[5] We brag about the diversity of our cities and the racial and ethnic harmony, but this has not always been the case.

In the nineteenth century, the Irish faced intolerance and prejudice. It was common to see signs advertising rooms to rent that said, "No Irish," or job listings reading, "No Irish Need Apply." The Irish were excluded from government jobs and business positions. Many were forced to work as manual labourers because those were the only jobs they could get. It took at least fifty years for this discrimination against the Irish to dissipate, and prejudice against Catholics lasted even longer.

In British Columbia, discrimination against immigrants from East Asia was even more entrenched. Chinese labourers were brought in to build the Canadian Pacific Railway through the mountains. They received low pay and faced unsafe working conditions. After 1885 Chinese immigrants were forced to pay a fifty-dollar head tax to come into the country. In 1900 this was raised to one hundred dollars and in 1903 raised again to five hundred dollars. Even this was not enough. After anti-Chinese riots in 1923, the Chinese Immigration Act (known today as the Chinese Exclusion Act) was passed, making it virtually impossible for Chinese to come into Canada. By the end of the 1920s, the population of Chinese was aging, and there were twelve to fifteen times more men than women.[6]

Sikhs were another target of discrimination. There was a small Sikh community in Vancouver prior to 1906. In 1914 a Japanese ship, the *Komagata Maru*, was chartered to sail from Calcutta to Vancouver. On board were 376 passengers, all but thirty of them Sikhs. Even though the ship violated no law, the passengers were not allowed to disembark once it reached Vancouver. For two months there were negotiations, but to no avail. The ship then returned to Calcutta. When it reached there the British authorities opened fire, killing eighteen and wounding twenty-five.[7]

Many Japanese settled on the west coast prior to the Second World War. A number were fishermen, and others worked in forestry and other industries. After the Pearl Harbor attack in November 1941, the federal government issued an order to intern all people of Japanese heritage; they were forcibly moved into the Interior, some as far away as Ontario. The internment lasted until 1949, four years after the war ended. Most of the Japanese lost property and were never compensated.

For over one hundred years Canada gave preference to immigrants of European ancestry. It was only in 1962 that Canada eliminated the overt racial discrimination of its immigration policy. In time attitudes changed, and other laws banning discrimination were passed. We became a more tolerant society, but prejudice and discrimination have remained.

Lesbian, gay, bisexual, and transgender individuals were forced to hide their sexual identity for decades. It was illegal to practise homosexuality. Some even went to jail. Finally, the law was changed. In 1969, then justice minister and attorney general Pierre Trudeau introduced legislation to decriminalize homosexuality. At the time he famously said, "There is no place for the state in the bedrooms of the nation."

But even this did not stop discrimination against and harassment of gays. On February 4, 1981, Toronto police raided bathhouses and broke down doors with crowbars and sledgehammers. Up to 250 were arrested that night. No one was ever convicted, but some people lost their jobs, and it ruined the reputations of others.

Discrimination of minorities has largely declined in this country, but the one group that continues to face major problems is young black men. Despite the laws, they still find it difficult to get work and rent apartments. Until recently, police in Toronto openly displayed racism by stopping young blacks for no apparent reason and demanding identification, a practice known as "carding." Again, it was the black community who spoke out against this practice. In time many others supported them and carding was ended.

But this issue is not over. Recently young blacks have protested under the banner Black Lives Matter. This is in protest of the shooting of blacks by police, not only in the United States, but also in Toronto.

* * *

THE YOUNG

To say the young are a special problem is nothing new. Problems for young people have been around at least since the time of Socrates, but there are several recent changes in Canada that indicate things are getting much more difficult for the young, or at least more difficult for young men.

One indication of all this is voting behaviour, and since we are talking about democracy, that is a good place to start. These are estimates of who went to the polls in the 2011 federal election by age and gender, provided by Elections Canada.

ESTIMATE OF VOTER TURNOUT BY AGE AND GENDER IN THE MAY 2, 2011, FEDERAL ELECTION[8]

Age	All	Males	Females
18–24	38.8	36.9	40.9
25–34	45.1	42.5	47.7
35–44	54.5	51.5	57.5
45–54	64.5	62.1	66.9
55–64	71.5	70.7	72.2
65–74	75.1	77.4	73.1
>75	60.3	69.5	54.2

Elections Canada, "Estimate of Voter Turnout by Age Group and Gender at the 2011 Federal Election."

When asked why they did not go out and vote, people give various excuses, like they did not have time or they were too busy. A better explanation is that they are alienated from the political process. They think voting makes no difference in their lives, or that their vote is meaningless. If voting is an indication of alienation, then these figures show that the young are far more alienated than older people, and younger males more than younger females.[9]

As an aside, the heavy voter turnout of older Canadians is a pattern that exists in all democracies. That is one of the reasons government policies tend to favour older people. They can swing elections.

So what are the social or political problems faced by young people? This generation is better educated than older people, but it is harder for them to enter the workforce. The young are facing a unique set of problems that is making it very difficult to get ahead. Youth unemployment is very high in several countries. In Greece it is 50 percent, in Italy it is 40 percent, and in Spain 47 percent. Canada's youth unemployment rate is 13.3 percent. In Toronto it is 18.1 percent. By contrast the Canadian unemployment rate is 6.9 percent.

Jobs are very scarce for young people with only a high school education, but even those with college and university degrees are finding it difficult. Over and over we hear of the underemployment of young people. These are people who cannot get the jobs for which they are trained; for example the university graduate working in a coffee shop or driving a taxi. Many are paying off student loans. Some have found it so difficult that they have returned home to live with their parents because they can't afford an apartment.

Part of the problem is that there simply aren't enough jobs. In 1976, 84.4 percent of men aged 26 to 64 were employed. By 2014 the rate of employment in this age group had fallen more than 10 percent to 74.2 percent, according to Statistics Canada. In that same period, the full-time employment rate for men aged 17 to 24 and who were out of school dropped by 18 percent. For men 25 to 29 it dropped by 10 percent. Most of that decline happened between 2007 and 2014, which includes the period now called the Great Recession.[10]

Employment for women of this age group is different. Many young women spend periods of time out of the workforce providing child care, but labour force statistics for women show that the full-time employment rate for those 25 to 29 has declined.

Is this solely the result of the Great Recession? Certainly that accounts for some of the job loss, but it is not the only reason. The offshoring of manufacturing to low wage countries is another. The introduction of robots at the workplace is another. Some analysts are saying a second technological revolution is upon us that will eliminate even more jobs. If the free trade agreements currently under review are passed, there will be an even greater loss of jobs, particularly unskilled and semi-skilled manufacturing jobs. All of this will make it more difficult for the young to get employment.

Corporations are converting many jobs from full-time to part-time in order to slash costs and increase profits. Part-time workers both reduce the cost of wages and save companies the expense of paying benefits. The median Canadian hourly wage is $23.08 for a full-time worker. For a part-time worker it is $13 an hour. Research by Toronto's United Way and McMaster

University found that about 52 percent of the workers in the GTA and Hamilton are in temporary, contract, or part-time positions. Virtually all of them have no benefits or job security, and many are working at low wage. Wayne Lewchuk, the lead researcher on the McMaster study, said, "This is the new form of employment."[11]

A government study in the United States found that 40.4 percent of the workforce were "contingent workers," defined as workers who work for an organization on a non-permanent basis.[12] This is the biggest job growth area in the U.S. economy. Like in Canada, most of those workers are suffering from low wages and few benefits.

Canada has shifted very rapidly to a service economy, which is encouraging part-time work. Today the goods-producing sector of the economy employs only 21.4 percent of the workforce, while services employ 78.2 percent. Manufacturing that once employed 30 percent of our workforce now employs only 9.4 percent. The largest sector of the workforce is retail at 15.1 percent, followed by health care and social assistance at 13.1 percent.

What has been happening is the slow decline of what were once considered traditional male jobs: agriculture, mining, forestry, construction, manufacturing, and transportation. After the Second World War many of these jobs became unionized and paid high wages. It is these jobs that are eroding. The jobs that are growing are in the service sector, like retail, food services, and hospitality. They are non-unionized and poorly paid with no benefits and no job security.

Chris Buckley, the president of the Ontario Federation of Labour, is outspoken about the shameful reality of the food service industry. "At nearly every stage of food production, from picking to packing to plating, there are appalling stories of vulnerable and precarious employees who barely earn enough to buy the food they serve."[13] The same could be said about many other jobs in the service sector.

We hear some voices protesting these changes and the harm that they are causing workers and the young. Most of the protesters are union leaders and academics; very few of them are workers or young people themselves.

We have pushed the young into the margins. They are becoming a lost generation. A crisis is building, and yet we do nothing.

* * *

PARTICIPATION OF THE EXCLUDED

To argue, as I have, that the excluded must become politicized, if they are to help themselves, is to tackle only one part of the argument. It is participation that is important. By engaging in the democratic process, our voices can be heard, and we can play our rightful role in our community and our country. It is the only way to bring change.

That is what the business community and the wealthy were able to do from the very beginning of representative democracy. It took much longer for unions and their members to be accepted and to participate in the democratic process, but once that happened, their role became an essential element of our democracy. It was different, again, for co-ops, non-profits, community groups, and environmentalists, but their participation was essential for the building of these movements.

The same is true for the poor, young people, aboriginals, minority groups, and many others. They have to become involved in the political process by participating. This is not only their right, but it is also the process by which they gain recognition, representation, and resolve their grievances. But how can they participate so their voices will be heard?

In Part 3 of this book we are going to go beyond what has happened in the past and the present to discuss what we can do in the future to become a truly participatory democracy.

PART 3

PARTICIPATORY DEMOCRACY

Canadians perceive their country as a place of liberal values, but we have a deeply conservative political culture. The major alliance is between government and the business or corporate elite. Unions, environmental groups, and community groups emerged to challenge this alliance but were put down, sometimes by force, more often by subtle but equally damaging means.

Despite this, grassroots organizations have continued to grow and are insisting that their concerns be met. A participatory democracy is emerging, but it still is resisted. That is the source of much of the political alienation. In Canada and the developed world, poll after poll has shown that people feel government is run by a few big interests, and everyone else has no say. They want to be involved in their communities and in the affairs of the country, and they want their government to listen to their concerns and find ways to act on them.

Elites claim that organizations controlled by ordinary people do not know enough to make good decisions. That is simply prejudice. The judgment of citizens and the organizations that represent them has been shown to be right again and again, while the advice that business provides is shaped by self-interest.

For decades, business supported by government fought unions, claiming it would be a disaster for their companies if workers had power, but when unions finally gained recognition, they proved to be responsible partners. The long battle over climate change finally resulted in the complete vindication of environmental groups, and the claims of the climate change deniers to be proven totally wrong. Community groups challenge new development, not to drive them away, but to make the development fit into their communities.

The alliance between government and big business has prevailed for over 150 years, and it is time to put it into retirement. We have a new way to go forward based on citizen participation, and we need a new arrangement between government and the people. Business has a role to play in that arrangement, but not a dominant role.

But how can 36.3 million Canadians transform politics so we become a participatory democracy? That is what we discuss in what follows.

CHAPTER 11

DEMOCRACY, PARTICIPATION, AND SOCIAL CHANGE

Some who advocate participatory democracy believe that once it is established the state will wither away and become a relic.[1] I don't believe that for a minute. We need an effective government that can make decisions, arbitrate between competing interests, set budgets, and all of the other practical things that must be done to manage our affairs. But we can only have good government, if the people are involved. The result will be an enriched democracy.

* * *

CHANGES IN CANADIAN SOCIETY

Canadian society has changed enormously since representative democracy was first introduced. In 1867, when Canada was founded, there were only four provinces. The west, the north, Prince Edward Island, and Newfoundland were not part of the country. The population was about 3.3 million people. Ontario had the largest number of people, with a population of 1.6 million; Quebec, 1.2 million; 387,000 in Nova Scotia; and 285,000 in New Brunswick. Most people lived in rural areas and small towns. The population of Montreal and its suburbs was 130,000. Toronto had 45,000 residents.

Nearly one million of Canada's population were French-speaking, about one-third of the total, and the remainder were English-speaking. New settlers came either from the United States or the United Kingdom, but about the same number of people that came into the country every year left, most going to the United States.

About 45 percent of the population was Catholic, and the rest were various Protestant denominations. Religion was very important in 1867, with high levels of church attendance. Churches had a conservative influence. In Quebec the Catholic Church encouraged people to live a rural life and have many children so their society could be protected from the overwhelming influence of the English. (This is called the "revenge of the cradle.")

Canada was largely a producer of staples. Forty-one percent of workers laboured on farms. The most productive agricultural areas were in Ontario and Quebec. Important crops were wheat, rye, oats, and potatoes. In Nova Scotia fishing and shipbuilding were dominant industries. The timber trade employed men primarily in the winter months in the Upper Ottawa Valley and the Miramichi Valley in New Brunswick. Most of the timber was exported to Britain.

Birth rates were high and life expectancy was short, resulting in a very young, growing population. Education levels were low, particularly in rural areas, but were improving. Cities and towns had schools, but they were private institutions and varied depending on the quality of the teachers. Parents had to pay fees to enroll their children in school. That meant many poor families could not afford to send their children to school. A number of universities had been founded. Almost all of them were church institutions. It was only after Confederation that provinces began to organize public education systems.

Men were the heads of family and the so-called breadwinners. The ideal was for women to be homemakers, but only middle- and upper-class families could afford to live that ideal. Rural women worked on farms, and in cities and towns women worked in various occupations, cleaning houses, in factories, or in small enterprises. Young women often worked as maids in the houses of affluent families. Many children worked full-time from the age of ten or younger.

There were about fifteen hundred miles of railway in Canada at the time of Confederation, but few people travelled far from their homes. Despite the proliferation of newspapers most were little more than propaganda sheets for political parties. This was a very insular society in 1867, and with the exception of a few professionals and those of means, people did not know a great deal about their own society and country, let alone the world.

A representative democratic system served a society like this fairly well. There were 180 seats in the first federal Parliament. On average, a constituency had less than 20,000 people, and only about one in eight could vote. Many voters knew their Member of Parliament personally, either through business or church.

The contrast between Canada of 1867 and the country today could not be sharper.

Canada had a population of 36.3 million people in 2016. The birth rate in 2012 was 1.61 births per woman, well below the rate needed to maintain current population levels. That is why today we accept about 300,000 immigrants and refugees every year. This has created one of the most ethnically diverse countries in the world. Over 20 percent of the Canadian population today is foreign born.

Average life expectancy in 2012 was 81.24 years. The retired population is large and growing rapidly. About 81 percent of Canadians live in cities. In 2011, the last full census, the Greater Toronto Area had a population of 6 million. By 2016 the population of the GTA had risen to almost 7 million; Montreal had 4.1 million; and Vancouver 2.4 million people. Many small towns and rural areas have smaller populations now than in 1867.

Canada is a post-industrial society with a GDP of two trillion dollars. We are a trading nation, very international in outlook. About 70 percent of our exports and 60 percent of our imports are with the United States. A highly diversified workforce is split with about 70 percent in service industries and 30 percent in goods production. Less than 2 percent work on farms.

The Canadian workforce is among the most highly educated in the world. Almost 75 percent of high school students go on to some form of post-secondary education.[2] Young people are staying in school longer and longer because training for jobs happens in schools. In 1867 most young people got only basic education, and job training happened at work.

Religion remains important but much less so than in the nineteenth century. As measured by church attendance, French Canadians are much less religious than the rest of the population.

Today there are 338 Members of Parliament. On average each parliamentary constituency has a population of 107,000 people. The vast majority of people do not personally know their MP. They cast their vote on the basis of the party or the leader of the party.

* * *

PARLIAMENT AND THE PEOPLE

Canadian society changed fundamentally between 1867 and today, and yet we continue to use the same political system of representative democracy. There have been reforms. The franchise has been expanded, and today we have universal suffrage. If some form of proportional representation is accepted, it will be a significant reform of the way that we select our politicians and will change the way that Parliament works, but it is still the same system of representative democracy.

Citizens have less control over their democratic institutions now than in the past because of the size of the population and the complexities of government. The majority of people have virtually no contact with their elected representatives, and yet they have more time to follow politics and are better educated and more informed.

Meanwhile the wealthy and the corporate elite continue to have enormous influence in our political process. They have excellent access to cabinet ministers, the real movers and shakers of government. This has happened in many developed countries. In the United States the corporations virtually write the laws and regulations that govern their businesses. It has not gone to that extreme in Canada, but big business continues to have undue power at all levels of government, and it reaps the rewards of favourable regulations and tax systems.

Parliament, in theory, is set up to listen to the public and respond with appropriate legislation, but it does not work that way. The party system is very rigid in Canada. Elected members follow the political lead of their party on all issues. Parliamentary committees are set up to examine legislation, but the committee system is weak. Again, party discipline is in force and ministers must follow the position of their party.

Citizens have the right to make deputations to parliamentary committees, expressing their concerns about the legislation under review, but in a rigid system like ours it is a frustrating experience. The politicians are not much interested in the deputations because they already know how they are going to vote on the issue. They are more interested in attacking each other than in listening to the citizen making the depuation. The press rarely reports on committees, and when they do it is shallow and perfunctory at best. Parliamentary committees are a show of public participation, not the real thing.

Is it any wonder that a large number of Canadians feel cynical about the practice of politics? They have been taught in school and told endlessly that this is a democratic country, but on public issues they have little opportunity to make a contribution. Their voices are ignored. In many ways, the message to citizens is that their views are unimportant.

But it is not only the practice of Parliament that excludes citizens from the political process.

* * *

CENTRALIZATION OF GOVERNMENT

What has happened in all developed countries is the creation of strong central governments. There are many reasons for this. The central government helps to unify the country, makes the regions more equal, develops transportation systems, promotes wealth and employment, provides for defence, enables and enforces the rule of law, and so on. Canadians support a strong federal government, but centralization has increased the loss of control by the people.

The seat of political power is a distance from where most people live. Bureaucracies run the day-to-day affairs of government, and they are remote and virtually impossible to influence. The real source of power is not our elected representatives; it is the prime minister and his or her staff, cabinet ministers, and senior bureaucrats. Even elected Members of Parliament have little power. Pierre Trudeau once said MPs were "nobodies fifty yards off Parliament Hill."

In the United States widespread resentment of Washington is distorting politics. The claim that a politician is "inside the beltway" is a curse. In Canada we talk about "western alienation" to express the anger toward the federal government in the western provinces. There is a sense that government is uninterested in them, and is spending their tax money in ways they do not support. It is mainly Conservatives who express this, but the feelings are shared by many of all political stripes across the country.

This problem of centralization is not only with our federal government. It can affect local government as well. It has happened in both Toronto and Montreal, our two largest cities.

*   *   *

CENTRALIZATION AND TWO CITIES

For forty-four years (1954–98), Toronto had a two-tiered municipal government. There were lower-tiered municipalities, like the City of Toronto, East York, Scarborough, North York, York, and Etobicoke, and the upper-tier Metropolitan Toronto ("Metro"). The system never worked very well, largely because it contained two different types of city: a downtown commercial district surrounded by densely populated older neighbourhoods, and the low-density suburbs.

Local governments within Metro adapted to this system in their own way. After 1971, with the election of a reform mayor and councillors, the City of Toronto developed a very progressive style of government by keeping Metro at arm's length. They brought development under control, established transparent decision making, and strengthened local communities. The suburbs approved more low-density developments and shopping malls, built wide roads for cars, and favoured expressways.

There were different proposals to solve this governance problem, but in 1998 the Mike Harris Conservative provincial government announced that they were going to amalgamate all of the Metro municipalities and create a new, one-tier City of Toronto, following the borders of Metro. The reason given for the reorganization was efficiency. Others say Harris wanted to kill the progressive style of government in the City of Toronto.

The reaction was immediate. Residents across Metro opposed the proposal because it would mean they would lose control over their local government. A large protest movement emerged, led by John Sewell, a former Toronto mayor, and Kathleen Wynne, later to become the Ontario premier. A referendum was held and three-quarters of the voters rejected amalgamation.

The Ontario government paid no attention to the wishes of the public and imposed amalgamation. Today the city has 2.8 million people. Council is made up of forty-four councillors elected in wards of more than fifty thousand residents, with one mayor elected at large. Since that time the reform movement has died. There are reform councillors from the old City of Toronto, but their votes are swamped by suburban councillors.

With the new structure of government, the people of Toronto have found it very difficult to shape the political process of their city. Like the committee system at the federal and provincial levels, public participation goes on, but it is ineffective and frustrating to citizens. Political life has been taken over by politicians and bureaucrats, and the people have little influence.

It does not have to be that way. This is another example of the reorganization of municipal government that had a much different result. In 2002 the municipalities on the Island of Montreal were merged into one megacity by the PQ provincial government. Again, the reason given was efficiency. Like in Toronto, this generated a huge controversy. People did not like it because they knew that this would result in a loss of control of their local government.

The controversy continued, and in 2004 a newly elected Liberal provincial government allowed referendums on the issue of municipal structure. After the referendum the province reorganized Montreal municipalities once again. In the final restructuring there is a mayor of Montreal elected at large, seventy-three councillors, an executive committee, and nineteen borough councils. In the reorganization what has emerged is a mix of centralized and decentralized governments.

It is the boroughs that are interesting. They are relatively small communities within Montreal. The largest has 165,000 people but most have around 50,000. Each borough has its own council, which has powers over planning, social and economic development, roads, culture, and community facilities. The boroughs control their own budget. This gives them considerable power, which they have used to bring in services and programs that are supported by the local people.

Le Plateau-Mont-Royal in Montreal is a downtown residential community north of Sherbrooke Street and east of Mont Royal. It has long been a cosmopolitan neighbourhood of French, English, and immigrants. Today it has come alive with restaurants, galleries, and small shops. Traffic is a problem, and the borough council has found ways to restrict the flow of cars and promote walking and the use of bike lanes.

The borough Côte-des-Neiges–Notre-Dame-de-Grâce has recently taken steps to restrict the number of fast food restaurants. A borough newsletter of eight to ten pages delivered to all residents has open discussions of issues. The borough has many other programs tailored to the needs of the community, including a partnership with a library for literacy programs in French, English, and other languages.

There is a sharp contrast between the way government operates in Montreal boroughs and in Toronto. The boroughs deliver local government supported by the residents. People identify with their borough as well as with the city of Montreal. There are enough councillors that they can often deal with constituents and their problems one on one. Toronto, by contrast, has become dominated by the concerns of suburbanites. Because of the size of the wards, it is difficult for people to get the attention of their councillors. Bike paths are fifteen years behind those of other municipalities, efforts to control traffic fail, and developers get their projects approved with cursory examination by council.

With government, size makes a huge difference. Can Ottawa, or the provincial governments, move their lumbering, clumsy, insensitive, bureaucratic form of government closer to the people? As Montreal demonstrated, it can be done.

Let me give two other examples where participation at a local level gives people greater control over their communities and results in better decision-making.

* * *

PARTICIPATORY BUDGETING

Participatory budgeting emerged out of the remarkable growth of democracy in South America in recent years. It began in Porto Alegre, a city in southern Brazil, in the late 1980s. Today, in that city, over 100,000 people participate in the budget process, most of them women from the poorest neighbourhoods.

What is little known is that there have been participatory budgeting experiments in Canadian cities such as Guelph, Hamilton, and Toronto. In

Hamilton's Ward 1, the local councillor, Brian McHattie, formed an advisory committee of twenty-one community members to decide how $1.6 million of city money would be spent in the ward. After considerable discussion the committee identified a number of projects including traffic lights, historical signage, public art, sidewalk repairs, speed bumps, a school lunch program, and others.[3]

The process is not complicated. In a participatory democracy, decisions are made through discussion, planning, and implementation. The volunteers listen to others and to the experts. Often they change their minds about elements of the project as they discuss the issues, and in the end they come up with detailed suggestions. The process is direct and it is conducted by local people, not through elected representatives. As much as possible important decisions are made by the people most affected by the decisions.[4]

This is the key to understanding participation and how it can create informed communities, increase the engagement of citizens, and change the way decisions are made. Meaningful, informed discussion deepens our understanding of issues, helps us to shape the forces of change, and leads to constructive decisions that are beneficial to everyone in the community.

Participation is a process of engagement that can change attitudes and beliefs. It is how people truly become involved in their community and help shape it for the better. It even helps those involved make new friends and understand the problems faced by their neighbours.

* * *

MIRVISH+GEHRY DEVELOPMENT

The planning process of Waterfront Toronto has already been described in chapter 9. This is a similar story, but it shows how citizens became involved in a complicated commercial and condominium development in downtown Toronto and helped the developer and the city resolve a difficult dispute. In the process, community members changed the project so that it became more acceptable to them.

In 2012, David Mirvish, son of the much-loved Ed Mirvish who built the iconic discount retail store Honest Ed's in Toronto, announced a new development on property he owned on King Street West. This was a massive new development that would take down almost a block of buildings across the street from Roy Thomson Hall and the Metro Hall. Three high-rise condo buildings would be built, each more than eighty storeys in height. The designer was Canadian-born architect Frank Gehry, who now lives in Los Angeles and is one of the leading celebrity architects in the world.

Immediately a controversy broke out. Among the detractors were restaurant owners further west on King Street. They said the new buildings would create wind tunnels and eliminate unique sight lines. They were concerned that it would take years to construct a project this size, and the construction would seriously disrupt their businesses. A meeting of local residents and property owners was held. David Mirvish attended and pointed out that the new development would bring huge benefits to Toronto. His collection of modern art would be housed in the new development. Frank Gehry's fame would also add to the prestige of the project. All of this would bring prestige to the city and benefit the cultural development of Toronto.

But the local residents at the meeting were not buying it. They complained about the traffic congestion that the huge condo development would bring to King Street. An increase in property taxes was another issue. It was pointed out that the streetcars were already overcrowded and this would make public transit even more congested. The height of the buildings was a problem for some, but it was the increased density that most residents complained about.

None of this stopped the development. Drawings were taken to the city by the developers and more problems came up. The planning department said that the new buildings did not fit into the character of the existing neighbourhood. They were concerned that the development would demolish four heritage buildings, but again it was the huge increase in densities that drew the most criticism.

The Mirvish+Gehry development had its supporters. Some talked about the boldness of the design, its unique quality, and the benefits to the city, but clearly there was a lot of concern from the public that the development would detract from this part of the city, and the densities would overload city services.

To deal with the controversy, Councillor Adam Vaughan organized a fourteen-member working group to see if a compromise could be worked out. After months of meetings and discussions among members of the committee, the city, David Mirvish, and Frank Gehry (or members of his staff), it was announced that a compromise had been reached that satisfied everyone, or at least most people.

The project was redesigned. Rather than three high-rise towers it was cut back to two, a 30 percent reduction, but one of the two buildings had escalated in height. The two towers were to be ninety-two and eighty-two storeys high. Both the city planning department and David Mirvish hailed the compromise as a great success.

Discussion and compromise by all of the parties had led to an agreement. If that had not happened the decision would have been referred to the Ontario Municipal Board, and all of the parties would be forced to accept their ruling.

* * *

BUREAUCRACY, POLITICIANS, AND THE PEOPLE

Modern governments are run on bureaucratic principles. It is the only way that large organizations employing huge numbers of people can be administered and controlled. But it can lead to various problems, not least of which is that it removes the people from control over their government.

The principles of bureaucracies are hierarchy, specialization, and administration run by impersonal rules. This allows for central decision making and the imposition of those decisions in an objective way on the entire bureaucracy and the people. It also leads to unwieldy organizations that are very resistant to change. Bureaucracies are top-down organizations, the very opposite of grassroots organizations.[5]

Canadian government bureaucracies are perhaps not as rigid as some, but they still present serious problems. The Stephen Harper government was the most centralized in recent memory. Virtually all major decisions were made either by Harper directly or by the Prime Minister's Office. Even cabinet ministers were often kept out of the decision-making process. The common complaint was that decisions were not so much arbitrary as they were made solely for political reasons.

Harper, for example, decided to cut the long form of the census. This was against the advice of researchers across the country and senior people in Statistics Canada. The reason given was that the long form was an invasion of people's privacy. Others said the government cancelled it because it revealed information they did not want made public. The prime minister did it anyway. There was an outcry from researchers and academics both in and out of government, saying that they needed the data to make good decisions on long-term plans. The PM refused to back down.

In another example, Harper ordered that all government scientists stop speaking to the press about the results of their research. The civil servants involved and the scientific community were up in arms. This violated one of the fundamental principles of science: open and critical discussion of research. This is a principle that was established as far back as the seventeenth century when the Catholic Church censored Galileo's scientific discoveries on astronomy. The prime minister did not care.

With the Harper government decisions were made in secret. The same was true for the Mike Harris Conservative government in Ontario. Maybe Conservatives are more secretive than others, but all governments make decisions behind closed doors and impose them by means of powerful bureaucracies.

This is a violation of our democratic principles. Government decisions should be made only after wide consultation. They should be transparent, and open to public criticism and scrutiny. How can we have government by the people if those with political power are not willing to listen to the opinions of the people?

* * *

PARTICIPATORY GOVERNMENT

Now more than at any other time in Canada's past, citizens want to be involved in public affairs. Today people follow political events and issues in detail. We have more leisure time. Rising levels of education have made the public more knowledgeable and less intimidated by government or by so-called experts. The media keeps us informed, and the internet gives us unprecedented information on a vast range of topics.

Today people can communicate with each other and with government easily and quickly through email, Facebook, Twitter, and other programs.

They want to participate and have the tools to do it in a meaningful way. A fundamental principle of government should be that all decisions must be open and transparent. There will be exceptions to this rule for privacy reasons, but open government is an essential rule.

The over-centralization of government has created serious problems because it shifts power to bureaucrats and politicians remote from communities. That eliminates control by citizens and hinders their ability to find local solutions to local problems. Of course, there are important decisions that must be made by a central body, but most decisions *can* and *should* be made at the local level.

We have to return to our democratic ideals and build a more open, egalitarian democracy where everyone participates to the best of their abilities. In the next chapter we discuss how we can build a participatory movement that is democratic to its grassroots.

CHAPTER 12

CREATING A PARTICIPATORY DEMOCRACY

In the aftermath of the U.S. presidential election in 2016 and the triumph of Donald Trump, there were a number of racist attacks on African Americans, Latinos, and Muslims. The election of a president with attitudes like Trump's gave legitimacy to anger and created the possibility of the expression of racism. This gives a new urgency to participatory democracy.

Divisions are inherent in modern, diverse societies because of differences of race, ethnicity, and religion. I have emphasized another division between economic elites and the rest of us. Politics can divide us but they can also be the way to unite us. I believe that if we can build a fairer, more egalitarian society where participation is encouraged and facilitated, it will unify us and make a stronger country. The way to do that is by building strong grassroots organizations that help people participate vigorously in public life.

What follows is a discussion of how we can finally introduce a real participatory democracy.

* * *

PARTICIPATION TODAY

We are on the brink of a participatory democracy. As I argued, that has emerged because our society has changed fundamentally. We are one of the most sophisticated, modern societies on the planet, with a highly educated population, aided by the most sophisticated communication technology available. The evidence is all around us that people want to be engaged in government. They want to participate, but how do we go the next step to create a participatory democracy?

We have talked a lot about grassroots organizations and how government works, but not that much about community control of government services. It might seem like a peripheral issue, and yet it is central to how people engage with their governments.

In Canada bureaucracies deliver government services; they employ welfare workers, children's aid societies, government inspectors, and so on. All of these agencies work in their own silos, and there seems to be little connection between them. The municipality does planning and picks up the garbage. The province delivers welfare cheques and provides education. The federal government supplies funds for Old Age Security and the Canada Pension Plan. What if all or some of those services were delivered by the community? That is what is happening in some cities.

* * *

WOODGREEN COMMUNITY SERVICES

Woodgreen is an independent, community-based social service organization. It operates in a working-class neighbourhood of more than one hundred thousand people in the east end of Toronto. The neighbourhood is in transition. Expanding pockets of affluence exist, but there is considerable poverty in its catchment area; most low-income residents gain their living by working at middle- or low-income jobs. Many of the older residents have sold their homes and younger families have moved in. Prices of houses have skyrocketed recently.

During the Depression, more than seventy years ago now, a United Church of Canada minister drew community members together to help meet the challenge of poverty, unemployment, and the problems of young people. In time that group evolved into Woodgreen Community Services. Forty years ago, Brian Smith, a young organizer, became executive director. His leadership, along with staff and a growing number of community volunteers, built it into the organization it is today.

Woodgreen receives some government funding because it runs a number of government programs in the community, but the organization is independent of government. Its community board manages the organization. The board sets policies, handles the finances, decides on new programs, and takes care of all the other details that are necessary for an organization of seven hundred full-time and part-time employees. It also runs a foundation and encourages community members to contribute financially to support the programs.

These are some of the services that Woodgreen provides. The organization runs seven daycare centres serving seven hundred preschool children. There are extensive programs for seniors ranging from social activities to income security programs and seniors housing. Woodgreen renovated an old hotel and uses it to house homeless men who were living on the street. Staff and volunteers help them to integrate into the community. Woodgreen administers seven hundred affordable housing units. There are several different types of youth programs, including a summer camp, homework clubs, English classes for immigrant children, a program for youths of African descent, and another for Muslim children. Recently, they helped six hundred Syrian refugee families settle into East Toronto. Woodgreen provides English as a second language classes. There are services for the mentally ill, programs for children with special needs, immigrant settlement programs, and a free tax clinic. A new program helps single mothers on welfare complete their education and get back into the workforce. These programs are run by professionally trained employees, but volunteers participate actively in most programs. The organization has not only survived, it has thrived. The benefits to the community cannot be estimated.

What is impressive is that Woodgreen is run by a board made up of community members, not the government. Those who say that local people cannot govern themselves know nothing about the vitality of community groups or of the skill of people working together to solve the problems of their neighbourhoods. If people are given the opportunity and the means, they can transform our communities, and make our cities more livable. That is grassroots participatory democracy at its best.

*   *   *

A NEW COMMUNITY-BASED MODEL FOR SERVICES

When I talked to people at Woodgreen, none of them seemed to understand that they have developed a new community-based model for the delivery of government services. They see it just as the logical way to deliver services needed by the residents, but it is much more than that. They have developed an agency delivering a sophisticated, comprehensive range of programs and services that is controlled by the community.

Some of its programs are funded by the government, and Woodgreen's staff write grant applications to maintain those programs. They must demonstrate that the funds are used properly, and provide regular reports. But they can handle that without any trouble. The organization does not deliver all government services in the community. Pension and welfare cheques arrive by mail.

Government does not interfere in the affairs of Woodgreen other than regular inspections. Because they are independent and community-run, the organization can work to meet all of the needs of the people in the community. They provide a decentralized, bureaucracy-free service that ends the dehumanizing centralization typical of most government agencies. In the process, this saves government money because it costs less to deliver services in this way.

Let's push the idea of decentralized, community-based services further. What if the province decided to move welfare services and provincial agencies like the Children's Aid Society into Woodgreen offices to deliver their services to the community. Perhaps the city, seeing all of these interesting things going on, might move some of their services out of city hall into the community. The police could set up a Woodgreen precinct and some of the officers could spend time working in the community youth programs, rather than monitoring them, looking for trouble. City planners could work with residents on neighbourhood planning issues, like traffic calming, better signage, new public benches in a retail area of the community, and so on. A planning exercise like this would be controlled by the residents, not the city planning department.

Perhaps other community groups within the Woodgreen catchment area could use its facilities? That might include the Rotary Club, a neighbourhood cycling organization, an environmental group, or a local union that wanted to hold its meetings there. No censorship — everything that is legal is allowed. If that were to happen, Woodgreen would be not only providing services, it would also be helping people participate.

If a developer decided to build multi-unit housing in the community, a locally controlled planning group could organize meetings of residents who live close by to discuss the project — not to criticize the design, but to ensure that the development meets the needs of the community. Developers are nervous about this type of participation because they are afraid the community will have unrealistic expectations, but this is how good development happens. Consultations are a process in which the different parties sincerely struggle to improve the project within the limits of budget and other restraints.

Community-based organizations, like Woodgreen, provide an opportunity to expand the control that residents have of their community, and to increase their ability to participate in issues that are important to them. They would lead to a strengthening of grassroots groups and facilitate the expansion of participatory democracy in an institution that the people already understand, and at the same time, bringing services and community groups together strengthens the community.

* * *

"CONFEDERATION OF COMMUNITIES"

The creation of broad public service organizations controlled by local people, like Woodgreen, would be an enormous step toward participatory democracy. It would help to create a structure so that people could make their voices heard in every neighbourhood and region in Canada. But there is still the enormous problem of citizens having effective control over country-wide issues, like taxation, justice, environmental controls, and all of the regulations that govern our lives and institutions. How can we effectively create a system where people can participate in issues on national, provincial, and municipal levels?

One idea proposed by Murray Bookchin, an American writer and activist, is building a "confederation of communities." The idea is simple but effective. Bookchin pointed out that the greatest problem hindering people from participating politically is that they are scattered across the country in separate communities. The governments, meanwhile, are concentrated in Ottawa and provincial capitals. They are insulated from the public by layers of bureaucracy. Municipal governments are closer to the people, but even they are difficult to influence, particularly in large cities.

These realities — the physical separation of government from the people and large bureaucracies — make it very difficult for the people to have influence in the hallways of power. Corporate leaders can easily break down those barriers, because they can travel to government capitals and they have enough prestige, money, and influence that politicians will meet with them and treat their concerns seriously. This is something that ordinary people find very difficult.

If there were a confederation of communities — a network of community organizations, like Woodgreen, across the country — it would provide the organizational structure for the voices of communities and local people to be heard. These groups could be located in inner cities, suburbs, towns, rural areas, First Nations reserves, and communities in the North. Even organizations like co-ops, non-profits, environmental groups, and unions could be linked together into confederations. All of these different communities could be connected online. They could share information, support each other in times of crisis, raise money for campaigns, and work together on political issues that impact everyone.

Computer technology has changed organizing and communication in this country, making it much easier. Information, such as research reports and magazine and newspaper articles, can be accessed online. Video and audio files can be distributed easily. Email can distribute a message to one person or to dozens. This creates an immediacy that would have been impossible back when people had to correspond by writing letters or relying on telephones.

I was on the National Council of the Writers' Union of Canada and later served as its chair. This is a Canada-wide organization, and members of the National Council live in every region of the country. All of the members are writers and computer literate; this made email our communication of choice. We had major debates by email, and even worked out a system where motions could be made, seconded, debated, and voted on, all online. This saved work, kept the group informed, and helped decision making in the union. Computer technology is making organization much easier.

A confederation of communities would achieve a couple of very important things. First, and perhaps most important, it would provide a forum for people across the country who are interested in particular issues to get to know each other and work together. Second, the group could organize how to take their concerns to the public in each community and reach a broader audience across the county.

One common tactic in working on new issues is to write a position paper. That requires research, talking to experts, interviews with people who are affected, meetings in communities, and so on. At the end of the process those involved at the community level will have deepened their understanding of the issue. Maybe some individuals in the group will change their opinions. That is all part of the process. But the group will then be very knowledgeable and can speak with authority on behalf of grassroots organizations and scores of people. In turn, that depth of knowledge and understanding gives the group status, prestige, and influence that can't be ignored. A confederation of communities, built on strong community organizations across the country, would be a very effective way to organize this process.

What follows are some examples from the past and the present — including successes and failures — that show different approaches to organizing.

* * *

BUILDING A CONSENSUS AROUND WELFARE REFORM

I mentioned that I worked for a welfare rights organization in Hamilton for a year during the 1970s. It was one of the defining moments in my career.

There were many administrative problems with the way welfare was administered by the City of Hamilton at that time. Recipients had to come into the office every month and wait, sometimes for hours, to see a welfare worker. There were complaints about mistreatment by the workers. Recipients were berated and some people were denied assistance for no reason other than they were disliked, or they had talked back to one of the workers.

To organize in a situation like this was risky and controversial, but it turned out to be relatively easy. We used the press effectively with some well-timed interviews of welfare recipients that appeared in the local newspaper. There was a sit-in of the welfare office that did not last long, but it was unsettling to the members of city council. We made lists of grievances, talked to politicians and anyone who would listen. In the end the politicians rejected virtually all of our demands, but things at the welfare office changed almost from the moment we started organizing. Recipients were treated with more respect, most were no longer required to come into the office every month, and the number of people denied assistance decreased dramatically. All this was accomplished in the first two or three months of the project. After that the welfare rights organization became a type of advocacy group defending individuals who had been denied support for one reason or another.

But the group was not satisfied, and as a young organizer I felt we had not done enough. We wanted to build a coalition that would improve the living standards of welfare recipients. That would mean connecting with other groups concerned about the administration of welfare across the province, because in Ontario the provincial government set welfare policies. From there the plan was to build a movement that had enough influence to change provincial policies across the country. It never happened.

The problem was that we did not have the organizational tools or knowledge to change the system. Welfare was administered by municipalities in Ontario. That meant that organizations of welfare recipients were focused on municipal, not provincial, welfare policies. We did not know how to make links with others concerned about welfare, and we had no idea how to develop a set of reforms that would make a difference. The obstacles were too many, and in the end, we had to be satisfied with the reform of the welfare practices in Hamilton.

* * *

CLIMATE CHANGE

If there has been one major success of participatory democracy in recent years, it has been the campaign on climate change. It provides a model of organizing that is very instructive.

There were many different groups and individuals that influenced this issue. A number of scientists recognized that this was a problem that could have devastating consequences, but it was activists in the environmental movement who mounted an effective campaign on climate change, reminding the public of an emergency that needed immediate attention. That put in motion other important elements.

In time, many in the scientific community were mobilized by the work of environmental groups. Detailed, rigorous scientific investigations were launched and once all of the data was gathered and examined, the conclusions confirmed what the environmental groups had been saying. Without the scientific work and the opinions of prominent scientists, it is unlikely that the politicians would have become involved. They had to put their reputations on the line if they were to support efforts to reduce climate change.

Of course, politicians were also very important in dealing with the issue. Canadians should pay special attention to how this issue was handled. During most of the 2000s, Prime Minister Stephen Harper did everything he could to keep climate change from becoming a major political issue in this country. Ultimately he failed, because the environmental movement kept it before the public, and for another reason: United States President Barack Obama. Obama led the effort that resulted in the international agreement on climate change at Paris.

The Paris Agreement is a victory of environmental groups and of citizen participation, but it also followed the type of organizational model of a confederation of communities proposed by Bookchin. The environmental groups in Canada and around the world were independent, but they shared the same information via the internet. The campaign to keep the issue before the public was not worked out in detail, but each group played its part in its own community and in the broader public discourse.

Every campaign is different, of course, but the campaign on climate change has elements that exist in many different campaigns: the participation of citizens, the role of experts, and, finally, the actions of politicians. In virtually all successful campaigns those elements are present.

The work of the scientists and environmentalists on climate change is now under threat, with the election of Donald Trump to the U.S. presidency, but he will have real problems rolling back this effort. Not only is there scientific proof that the climate change crisis was caused by the burning of fossil fuels, but there is also a strong and mobilized environmental movement ready to act if Trump tries to dismantle the Paris Agreement.

* * *

INCOME INEQUALITY AND TAX HAVENS

Income inequality and the sheltering of money in tax havens is another issue that will be difficult to solve. The only way this issue can be dealt with effectively is by using the tax system to redistribute income, closing the many tax loopholes, and making it impossible to offshore money in order to avoid paying taxes. This is easy to say, but it will be difficult to do because there must be a broad consensus, and pressure from the grassroots, to make politicians act.

The tax regime in this country and others is incredibly complicated. Corporations and those with high incomes will fight hard to retain their privileges. Tax and income inequality speak to the core values of our capitalist society. Some level of inequality is expected, but what is appropriate? Everyone has a different opinion. Taxes have been used as an economic stimulus for certain sectors of the economy, and as a way to discourage consumption. For example, tax concessions were given to stimulate the oil industry, and concern about health has led to taxes being levied on tobacco and alcohol as a way to reduce sales. These complications and the broad impact of taxes are why politicians are very reluctant to consider a major overhaul of the system, but if the problems of income and social inequality are to be addressed, the challenge must be taken up.

We have already looked at income inequality and tax avoidance schemes in chapter 4. There is no need to repeat it here. What is important is to discuss how we can establish an effective strategy to bring changes to our tax policies. Let's begin when it first became a major controversy.

In September 2011 a group of young people gathered on New York streets to create the Occupy Wall Street movement. "We are the 99 percent," was their most effective slogan, dramatizing the fact that the richest 1 percent of the population were making huge incomes while the incomes of everyone else were stagnant or falling. Soon there were Occupy movements in major cities around the world, including Toronto, Montreal, and Vancouver. But on November 15 the New York police moved against the protesters and cleared Zuccotti Park. The protests went on until February 2012, when they petered out. The organizers were not able to build a lasting grassroots movement.

But this was not the end of the controversy. After the collapse of the demonstrations, researchers began to focus on the issue of income inequality. In this country that was done most effectively by the Canadian Centre for Policy Alternatives. Even well-regarded economists like Joseph Stiglitz spoke out, saying that increasing income inequality poses a serious risk to the economy because it is lowering consumer demand.

Some political action resulted. In Canada there has been an increase in the tax rate of top-income earners, but it will not be enough to solve the income inequality problem. In the U.S. presidential election Hilary Clinton promised to increase the tax rate for those earning over $250,000. Her defeat ended that proposal, and Donald Trump could well increase the tax cuts to the wealthy, making the problem even worse in that country.

The only way to bring change on this vital issue is to build a cross-country movement for reform of our tax regime in Canada. A confederation of communities would be an effective network to take up this campaign, but it does not yet exist and so the issue languishes.

If there were strong grassroots support and effective organization, it would not be difficult to develop a strategy for change. In the past, Royal Commissions have been formed to study complicated issues like tax reform. That could be one political demand. If that does not work, then grassroots groups could establish their own commission. Let's suggest a name: "A People's Commission on Income Inequality and Taxes." Broad commissions like this publicize the issues, make the case for reform, and provide detailed suggestions for resolving the issue.

Unless a grassroots movement with broad public support can execute a strategy to make income inequality, taxation, and tax havens into a public controversy, nothing will happen.

* * *

PARTICIPATION AND DEMOCRACY

These are only some of the most pressing issues that we face. There are many others.

The problems of First Nations have now taken centre stage in Canada and there is reason to be optimistic. Aboriginal people are mobilizing and have developed an effective movement, demanding change. Their goals are to raise living standards and strengthen aboriginal culture. They have a strategy and will execute it. I expect there will be militant action, angry meetings, and confrontations. It will take time, but First Nations people will look after themselves. The most the rest of us can do is support their efforts.

The problems associated with low wage service workers are quite different. More and more people are caught up in these types of jobs, many of them young, and they are becoming increasingly frustrated. In this case, there is a strong organization that could lead this cause: the trade union movement. In the Depression years of the 1930s and the war years of the 1940s unionists built the labour movement. They moved millions of workers and their families out of poverty and into the middle class. This helped to turn Canada into a prosperous country. Low-paid service workers can do the same, and if unions became involved in that struggle it would help to rejuvenate the labour movement.

Still other pressing issues are the free trade agreements that have been signed. Even more are being proposed. Corporations have been consulted extensively, but very few ordinary people have been involved in this process. This must change. The recent election in the United States has shown how many people are deeply concerned because they feel their jobs and their way of life are threatened. Similar concerns are felt by Canadians. Only when the people become involved in this process, and when the agreements benefit all of the people, will they be accepted.

The anger that we see infecting public life in many other countries — including our own — comes down to this: representative democracy does not work very well because it favours some people and not others. Democracy is not simply casting a vote every four years. It should be seen as an ongoing process in which people can participate in the public issues that concern them and government decisions reflect those concerns.

* * *

ORGANIZING FOR DEMOCRACY

This has been a discussion of how to set up an organizational structure so that citizens — ordinary people — can develop a consensus on important political issues and move toward implementing that consensus politically.

These are ideas that I have developed in the years that I have been involved in grassroots organizations. Others will have even better ideas of how to mobilize people around issues. That is the way that organizing works. New ideas feed on old ideas, and we move forward.

But for this to happen we have to develop grassroots organizations that can facilitate the process. That is what our history teaches us. Charismatic leaders or political parties will not bring the changes we need. They will come from the grassroots, and these organizations will not appear magically. They will be created by people dedicated to helping us find our political voice. It can happen; it must happen if we are going to be a truly democratic country.

Our system of representative democracy is in deep trouble. Corporations and the self-interest of the 1 percent dominate our government. They have established a political and economic system for their own interests. Like people in the United States and the rest of the developed world, Canadians are uneasy. If we don't balance the "louder voices" with policies that have the support of the people, there will be nothing but trouble ahead.

There are dangers, of course. The Trump victory was won with simplistic, dishonest promises: deport illegal immigrants, demolish the trade deals, bring back the jobs. Slogans like those are designed to confuse the public and win votes. They are lies that do not reflect the legitimate problems that we face, and cannot be implemented. This is demagoguery.

I have confidence in the people. Participatory democracy depends on discussion, information, research, and focus on the real problems, not fantasy solutions and false promises. It is by participation and a genuine attempt to understand issues and find solutions that answers emerge. This takes hard work by scores of people in the grassroots, but it is the best way forward.

In the end, participatory democracy is reformist, not revolutionary. We still need politicians, parliaments, city councils, and all of the apparatus that surrounds government. There will still be elections when we argue and debate about what is best for our country. That is an important part of the fabric of our country and our public life. But we must build a participatory democracy if we are to achieve the great ideal of "government of the people, by the people, for the people."[1]

APPENDIX
Some Rules for Reformers[1]

In writing this book I made notes based on my experience with various grassroots organizations over the years. I intended to put them somewhere in the last couple of chapters, but they would not fit with the flow of the argument. I offer them here in the hope that those in the trenches of organizing might find them useful.

THE NATURE OF GRASSROOTS

Grassroots organizations are groups of equals in which everyone is encouraged to participate. Members might be different in terms of experience and education, but everyone in the group is on the same level.

This is a simple principle, but sometimes it is difficult to put into practice. The leaders of the organization have greater knowledge about the issue than others because of their involvement, but each of them is only one member of the group.

Always structure grassroots organizations on democratic principles. The decisions made are decisions of the group.

INFORMATION, INFORMATION, INFORMATION

Information is the currency of any grassroots organization. There should be no secrets. Keeping members of a group informed is essential; it helps to keep them motivated and creates a path to good decisions.

Disseminating information to members is something community groups are getting much better at with home computers. Working in grassroots organizations prior to the 1990s meant you had to spend an inordinate amount of time on the telephone trying to keep people informed about meetings and events. Email has simplified and streamlined that effort tremendously. Today it is hard to participate meaningfully in an active community group without a home computer.

Because of its immediacy I am a great believer in electronic communication, but in some cases the old way of doing things works best. For instance, there is often a need for a printed newsletter. In my community, Toronto Island, newsletters are distributed in mailboxes because some people are not online, but the other reason is that having a paper copy of something increases the likelihood that it will be read. Many union locals still hand out newsletters and flyers at the plant gates for the same reason. There is a much better chance that they will be read by members during coffee breaks and lunch.

OUTREACH

It isn't only members of the group who need to be kept informed. Communicating to the public is essential for most grassroots organizations. Outreach should be a central strategy of every group.

The spokesperson is the public face of the organization, and he or she should be chosen carefully. The spokesperson should be a good communicator, have a command of the issue, be able to deal with the media confidently and effectively, and be able think on his or her feet.

Press conferences at one time were a preferred way to deliver a message, but they are used less and less by groups because it is hard to get the attention of the media. This is particularly true in a city like Toronto where there are a lot of news outlets. The press release delivered by email often is a better tool. A message can be crafted that clearly describes the issue. Including the name and contact information of the spokesperson is essential to a press release. If a media person wants more information, they will call.

A grassroots group needs a website to describe the history of the group, its objectives, and how to contact the group. Many websites are equipped to host blogs in an effort to encourage public discussion of issues. Others link to Facebook and Twitter accounts.

I am a writer and it took me a long time to learn that a picture is worth a thousand words. Use photos and illustrations as much as possible. That draws eyes to the site.

SLAPP SUITS

Community activists often worry about threats of legal action — either against the group as a whole or against an individual. This is rare but it does happen.

Some legal actions are launched to attack community groups and critics in order to silence them. They are called SLAPP Suits — Strategic Lawsuits Against Public Participation. They are designed to intimidate or silence critics by burdening them with the often crippling expense of mounting a legal defence.

In Canada, only Ontario and Quebec have anti-SLAPP legislation. The Ontario legislation allows for a fast-track application for dismissal on the basis that the suit is without merit.

Any spokesperson needs to be careful when speaking for a group. Be sure all facts are accurate and any opinions are based on those facts. For example, don't say that one of your adversaries is dishonest unless you have proof or strong evidence of dishonesty. Even then it might be difficult to prove in court. Assume your opposition is honest, but misguided, and you are on safer ground.

DO NOT GET CAPTURED BY OTHERS

Many members of unions, environmental groups, and community groups are also members of established political parties. Normally this shouldn't be a problem. However, if your group becomes too closely identified with one particular party or politician, members of other political parties may dismiss your issue.

The safest rule is to keep a respectable distance from political parties, corporations, and others. If a politician endorses the position of the group, that is fine, but don't get too cozy.

DEVELOP A STRATEGY

The most important element of a strategy is realism. If there is no way that a group can achieve its objective, then the strategy has set the group up for failure. Here are a few ideas to help prevent that from happening.

Stay informed: Listen to what politicians, the media, other citizens' groups, and individuals are saying about your issue. Counter their opinions with facts and arguments founded on good information. For example, in the fight against the Island Airport some opponents would say they liked the convenience it provided. We would agree, but counter that argument by saying the planes were degrading Toronto's waterfront, which is in the process of being redeveloped. Thousands of people will be living and working in new waterfront communities. A busy airport is incompatible with that redevelopment. Toronto has an excellent airport, Pearson, and air traffic from the Island Airport should be relocated there.

Public meetings: Public meetings are very important. They are an opportunity to explain the point of view of the members of the group, and if the issue has a profile it will attract publicity. Encourage as many of your members as possible to speak at these meetings. Explain that they should identify themselves as a member of the group, but give their own comments.

Their knowledge and passion will surprise everyone. Nothing improves morale and encourages solidarity more than having members of the group explaining their point of view in public meetings.

Demand transparency: The group needs to see all pertinent documents. This demand will often be resisted — but ask anyway. You can only judge whether a document is important after you see it.

Governments are required to make documents and correspondence public if requested. Often, however, the material is redacted with heavy black ink.

Find support for your issue with local politicians: Keep the politicians engaged in your issue informed about what is happening. If, for example, your issue is coming to council, see if your councillor will set up meetings with other councillors so that members of the group can explain their position to them. Lobbying is still very important in the world of politics.

Ask for consultations: I believe there should be consultations on most issues. Make the opposition understand they are dealing with people concerned about their community or the impact of the issue on their members. Consultation is also the best way to get information and, hopefully, to resolve issues before they become problems.

In community organizations consultations are particularly import-ant. Whenever a new building is proposed in an existing community there should be full consultations between the developers and their staff and the neighbours. Secrecy and the unexpected cause many problems.

Using advisors: Sometimes the information that groups come across can be very technical, and it is best to have advisors who can help with analysis.

Trade union locals, in my experience, are well served by the research departments of their unions when it comes to negotiations, but there may be special issues in particular plants that pose health risks. Workers handling toxic materials like asbestos or paints should be given special instructions and protective equipment, if necessary. Safety is a very important issue on construction sites and in some manufacturing plants.

There are experts that can help local unions on all of these issues, and sometimes it is worth getting outside help even if it costs money or annoys the union research department.

Expect the unexpected: In organizing, the best opportunities always seem to emerge unexpectedly. Keep your strategy flexible because the cir-cumstances, and even the issue, may change.

CONFRONTATION

Sometimes compromise and discussions are hopeless, and it comes to con-frontation. In British Columbia, for example, the struggle by environment-alists to preserve old-growth forest became a demand that the provincial government change its forest management policies. When the government refused, the environmentalists had two choices: they could either back off or mount protests. They decided on protests.

The environmentalists had an effective publicity campaign that drew wide public support for saving the old-growth forests. Then a series of demonstrations were mounted, including picketing, stopping logging trucks, and so on. In time their objectives came to be supported by unlikely groups like the chamber of commerce and local councils in nearby towns and municipalities. Ultimately the B.C. government agreed to change their policy and save the old-growth forests.

In mounting militant action, the cardinal rule is no violence because that will lose you public support. If the police are called in, things can quickly turn ugly. If there are arrests, the group should never abandon those who get into trouble. Everyone is in the struggle together. "Hang together or you will hang alone" is an apt organizer's slogan.

BUILD THE SOLIDARITY OF THE GROUP

Members should feel that they are both part of a movement and contributing to it. The level of involvement will vary. For some, attending a meeting and listening will be enough; others will want more engagement. Members must *at a minimum* be given the opportunity to talk at meetings, even if their views differ from the majority. By participating, they are making a contribution to the group.

They might also be given a task like writing a piece for the group's blog, or becoming a member of a committee designing a flyer. That helps them identify with the group.

The social side to meetings helps people get to know others in the group. It creates a bond and often, friendships. In our fight against the Island Airport we always made a point to invite everyone out for a drink after meetings. It wasn't much, but for all of us, especially newcomers, it helped to bind us together as a strong group. Many of those people remain close friends of mine.

Pay attention to the social side of organizations.

ACKNOWLEDGEMENTS

Many people helped to shape my understanding of politics and the importance of participation: Brian Iler, Alan Sparrow, Sue Sparrow, Marc Brien, Bob Kotyk, Barry Lipton, Anshul Kapoor, Ron Jenkins, and others.

Let me mention some others who were important to me: David Harris, Alec Farquhar, John Restakis, Dick Nielsen, Wendy Loten, Jim Lorimer, John Sewell, Olivia Chow, Brian Smith, and Adam Vaughan.

Special thanks to my editors and the people at Dundurn Press: Dominic Farrell, Carrie Gleason, Cheryl Hawley, and the publisher, Kirk Howard.

Finally, thanks to my partner, Paulette Pelletier-Kelly, who put up with all my impatience and frustrations in the writing of this book.

I have been a writer for a long time, and creating a book has never been easy. *Democracy Rising* will have a special place for me because it allowed me to write about participation in various kinds of groups, something that I have done all of my adult life. Thank you for taking the time to read my thoughts, ideas, reflections, and conclusions. I hope you found them of interest.

NOTES

CHAPTER 1: REPRESENTATIVE DEMOCRACY

1. Thomas Jefferson on politics and government, http://famguardian.org/Subjects/Politics/thomasjefferson/jeff1350.htm.
2. Eric Evans, "A British Revolution in the Nineteenth Century," *BBC History*, 2011, www.bbc.co.uk/history/british/empire_seapower/revolution_01.shtml.
3. Allan Greer, *The Patriots and the People: The Rebellion of 1837 in Rural Lower Canada* (Toronto: University of Toronto Press, 1993).
4. There are a number of excellent books on the 1837 revolt and more than one play. The book I like is William Kilbourn, *The Firebrand: William Lyon Mackenzie and the Rebellion in Upper Canada* (Toronto: Clarke, Irwin, 1956).

CHAPTER 2: ELECTIONS AND UNIVERSAL SUFFRAGE

1. An excellent description of the different qualifications for the right to vote can be found in the Elections Canada website. Elections Canada, "A History of the Vote in Canada," www.elections.ca/content.aspx?section=res&dir=his&document=chap2&lang=e.
2. Ibid., chapter 2.
3. Ibid., chapter 2.
4. Brent Patterson, "Ranked Ballots Would Have Given the Liberals 224 Seats this Past Election," Council of Canadians Acting for Social Justice, http://canadians.org/blog/ranked-ballots-would-have-given-liberals-224-seats-past-election.

CHAPTER 3: DEMOCRACY AND THE RISE OF CANADIAN CAPITALISM

1.   John Douglas Belshaw, *Canadian History: Pre-Confederation*, https:// opentextbc.ca/preconfederation/chapter/6.

2.   I have written more extensively about the Great Western Railway. Bill Freeman, "Welfare Hamilton Style," in *Their Town: The Mafia, the Media and the Party Machine*, eds. Bill Freeman and Marsha Hewitt (Toronto: James Lorimer, 1979).

3.   Thirty-five years ago I researched and wrote about the municipal subsidies in Hamilton. It was then that I came to understand the massive subsidies given to business by government. That is the genesis of this chapter on subsidies in this book and the ideas around elite control of the political process. What is new in my thinking are the ideas around participatory democracy. That comes out of years of participating in various groups. This is the reference to the material on municipal subsidies in Hamilton. Bill Freeman, "Welfare Hamilton Style," *Their Town*, 19–23.

4.   William Kilbourn, *The Elements Combined: A History of the Steel Company of Canada* (Toronto: Clark, Irwin, 1960), 39.

5.   David Russell, "A Financial History of Hamilton" (B.A. Thesis, McMaster University, 1936), 48.

6.   Kilbourn, *The Elements Combined*, 48.

7.   Russell, "A Financial History," 46.

8.   "International Harvester," 1920, Hamilton Public Library, newspaper clipping files.

9.   Russell, "A Financial History," 47.

10. Ibid., 48.

11. Mark Milke, "Corporate Welfare at Industry Canada since John Diefenbaker," Fraser Institute, July 2013, www.fraserinstitute.org/sites/ default/files/corporate-welfare-at-industry-canada-since-john-diefenbaker-rev.pdf.

12. Tamsin McMahon, "Why Corporate Welfare Doesn't Boost Employment," *Maclean's*, February 6, 2014.

13. McMahon, "Corporate Welfare."

14. Ibid.

15. IMF survey, "Counting the Cost of Energy Subsidies," July 17, 2015, www. imf.org/external/pubs/ft/survey/so/2015/NEW070215A.htm.

CHAPTER 4: ELITE CONTROL IN A DEMOCRATIC SYSTEM

1. Adam Smith, *An Enquiry into the Nature and Causes of the Wealth of Nations*, 1776. Self-interest has long been discussed by social philosophers. For a good review of the issue see David O. Sears and Carolyn L. Funk, "The Role of Self-Interest in Social and Political Attitudes," *Advances in Experimental Social Psychology*, 24 (1991): 2–80.

2. The story of the Pacific Scandal has been told many times in books and articles. This is a good summary: www.thecanadianencyclopedia.ca/en/article/pacific-scandal/.

3. John Ibbitson, "PM to Ban Donations by Unions, Companies," *Globe and Mail*, December 20, 2002.

4. "Quebec's Elections Watchdog Tallies Toll of Political Donation Scheme," *Globe and Mail*, April 3, 2013.

5. Martin Regg Cohn, "Revealed: The Secret Price of Admission to Power," *Toronto Star*, March 29, 2016.

6. "In Ontario and B.C., Access Is on Sale," *Globe and Mail*, March 29, 2016.

7. Martin Regg Cohn, "Done Like Dinner: Corporate and Union Donations," *Toronto Star*, March 30, 2016.

8. Gary Mason, "Pricey Political Fundraisers Elicit Big Cash and Concerns," *Globe and Mail*, March 30, 2016.

9. Justin Hunter and Adrian Morrow, "Clark Promises Fundraising Transparency," *Globe and Mail*, April 1, 2016.

10. Robert Fife and Steven Chase, "Morneau Fundraiser One of a List of Liberal Cash-For-Access Events," *Globe and Mail*, October 20, 2016.

11. Canadian Centre for Policy Alternatives, *Alternative Federal Budget, 2016*, 25, www.policyalternatives.ca/sites/default/files/uploads/publications/National%20Office/2016/03/AFB2016_Main_Document.pdf.

12. David Macdonald, "Out of the Shadows," Canadian Centre for Policy Alternatives, November 2016, www.policyalternatives.ca/sites/default/files/uploads/publications/National%20Office/2016/11/Out_of_the_Shadows.pdf.

13. CCPA, *Alternative Federal Budget, 2016*, 98.

14. Harry Kitchen, "The Return of the Gilded Age: Consequences, Causes and Solutions," Broadbent Institute, 2015.

15. Eric Reguly, "Stuck in the Middle with Taxes," *Globe and Mail*, May 28, 2016.

16. "Stock Options: Outrageous Corporate Freebies," *Canadians for Tax Fairness*, www.taxfairness.ca/sites/taxfairness.ca/files/factsheets/stock-option-factsheet-april2_3.pdf.

17. "Canadian $$ in Tax Havens Reach $199 Billion," www.taxfairness.ca/en/news/canadian-tax-havens-reach-199-billion.

18. "Oxfam Says Wealthiest 1 Percent Richer Than Rest of World Population," *Radio Free Europe/Radio Liberty*, www.rferl.org/content/poverty-wealth-inequality/27493727.html.

19. "Huge Cost of Tax Evasion Revealed as Campaign to Tackle Tax Havens Launches," Canadians for Tax Fairness, www.taxfairness.ca/en/news/huge-cost-tax-evasion-revealed-campaign-tackle-tax-havens-launches.

20. Tanya Talaga, "Tax-Haven Deals had Ottawa's Blessing," *The Toronto Star*, June 18, 2016.

21. "Get On With the Review," *Globe and Mail*, June 20, 2016.

22. Aditya Chakrabortty, "The 1% Hide Their Money Offshore — Then Use It to Corrupt Our Democracy," www.theguardian.com/news/commentisfree/2016/apr/10/money-offshore-corrupt-democracy-political.

CHAPTER 5: TOP-DOWN REFORM: PROGRESSIVES AND THE FARM PARTIES

1. The most colourful book describing a political machine is William L. Riordon, *Plunkitt of Tammany Hall, A Series of Very Plain Talks on Very Practical Politics* (New York: Dutton, 1963).

2. Statistics Canada, *Canada Year Book*, 1932.

3. U.S. Bureau of Census, internet release date June 15, 1998.

4. For the full text of the Regina Manifesto see: www.connexions.org/CxLibrary/Docs/CX5373-ReginaManifesto.htm.

CHAPTER 6: TRADE UNIONS

1. There are many fine books and articles about unions and working conditions in Canada. I have written extensively about unions in Hamilton in both the nineteenth and twentieth centuries. *Glory Days*, a play I wrote about the 1946 Stelco strike, was produced twice by Hamilton's Theatre Aquarius. For material on the early history in this chapter I have relied on Bryan D. Palmer's *Working-Class Experience*. It provides historical information on unions, business history, and working conditions. Bryan D. Palmer, *Working-Class Experience: the Rise and Reconstitution of Canadian Labour, 1800–1980* (Toronto: Butterworth, 1983).

2. Palmer, *Working-Class Experience*, 30.

3. Ibid., 99.

4. Ibid., 97.

5. Ibid., 153.

6. There are a number of excellent accounts of the Winnipeg General Strike. See particularly David Bercuson, *Confrontation at Winnipeg: Labour, Industrial Relations, and the General Strike* (Montreal: McGill Queen's University Press, 1990).

7. Palmer, *Working-Class Experience*, 176.

8. "The GM Oshawa Strike 1937," http://socserv.mcmaster.ca/ oldlabourstudies/onlinelearning/cawhistory/essays/essay7.html.

9. "The Ford Windsor Strike, 1945," http://socserv.mcmaster.ca/ oldlabourstudies/onlinelearning/cawhistory/essays/essay5a.html.

10. My book *1005: Political Life in a Union Local* includes a chapter on the 1946 Stelco strike. It also describes the politics of the union, negotiations, and the grievance system. I have drawn on that research for this book. This is the full reference. Bill Freeman, *1005: Political Life in a Union Local* (Toronto: James Lorimer, 1982).

11. "Striking Facts: Working Days Lost to Labour Disputes," *Economist*, www.economist.com/node/16976532.

12. "Key Labour and Income Facts," *Perspectives on Labour and Income*, www.statcan.gc.ca/pub/75-001-x/00801/5881-eng.html#Ref_HRDC_2001.

13. At the time of publication of *Democracy Rising*, Local 1005 had a membership of only 650.

CHAPTER 7: CO-OPERATIVES AND THE SOCIAL ECONOMY

1. John Restakis, "Defining the Social Economy: The B.C. Context," BC Social Economy Roundtable, www.msvu.ca/socialeconomyatlantic/pdfs/ DefiningSocialEconomy_FnlJan1906.pdf.

2. This site provides a good description of the history of the British co-operative movement: www.wow.com/wiki/British_co-operative_movement.

3. "Rochdale Principles," www.wow.com/wiki/Rochdale_Principles.

4. The Canadian Worker Co-op Federation website is: http://canadian worker.coop.

5. Ian MacPherson, "The History of the Canadian Co-operative Movement: A Summary, a Little Historiography, and Some Issues," 4, http://socialeconomyhub.ca/content/telelearning-session-19-long-view-social-economy.

6. There are many sources of information about the Fishermen's Protective Union. This citation is from the Memorial University Maritime History Archive: www.mun.ca/mha/fpu/fpu18.php.

7. "B.C. Fishermen's Co-operative Association," Centre for Co-operative and Community-Based Economy, www.uvic.ca/research/centres/cccbe/resources/galleria/stories/BCFishermensCooperativeAssociation.php.

8. The information about the Coady International Institute comes from an interview I had with Olga Gladkikh, who taught at the Institute. http://coadyextension.stfx.ca.

9. "Cooperative Housing in Canada," ICA Housing, www.chfcanada.coop/icahousing/pages/membersearch.asp?op=country&id=2.

10. Arctic Co-operative Limited, www.arcticco-op.com/index.htm. Other information in this section came from an interview with CEO Andy Morrison in 2006.

11. This information comes from Co-op Atlantic, www.coopatlantic.ca, and interviews with Brian Inglis and co-op members in Cheticamp.

12. Vancity, www.vancity.com. This information also comes from an interview with Bob Williams held in 2006.

13. This information comes from Mountain Equipment Co-op, www.mec.ca/en, and an interview with Peter Van ter Weeme and Tim Southam.

14. SolarShare, www.solarbonds.ca Additional information has been provided by Brian Iler.

15. Canadian Co-operative Association, www.coopscanada.coop/en/international_dev/about.

CHAPTER 8: THE ENVIRONMENTAL MOVEMENT

1. I am indebted to Laurel Sefton MacDowell for some of the details in this chapter on the environment. It goes well beyond my chapter, which focuses only on the environmental movement. This is the reference to her book. Laurel Sefton MacDowell, *An Environmental History of Canada* (Vancouver: University of British Columbia Press, 2012).

2. Pollution Probe, www.pollutionprobe.org.

3. Greenpeace Canada, www.greenpeace.org/canada/en/home. Greenpeace International, www.greenpeace.org/international/en.

4. Pembina Institute, www.pembina.org.

5. David Suzuki Foundation, www.davidsuzuki.org.

6. GoodWork.ca, Canada's Green Job Site, www.goodwork.ca/environmental-groups.

7. The book *Merchants of Doubt*, and later the film and website by the same name, show how major corporations entered into a scheme to deny the scientific evidence of the harmful effects of cigarette smoking and greenhouse

gas emissions. They did this to suppress the evidence and maintain high profits. www.merchantsofdoubt.org.

8. Intergovernmental Panel on Climate Change, *Climate Change 2013*, www.ipcc.ch/pdf/assessment-report/ar5/wg1/WGIAR5_SPM_brochure_en.pdf.

9. The Leap Manifesto, https://leapmanifesto.org/en/the-leap-manifesto/#manifesto-content.

CHAPTER 9: COMMUNITY GROUPS

1. Government regulations have tended to make groups more formal. In order to open a bank account a group must be incorporated.

2. The Syrian civil war started as a protest movement of Sunnis for greater freedoms during the Arab Spring of 2011. The protesters also called for the resignation of the government of Bashar al-Assad. The government used military force to try and crush the movement, resistance emerged, and the civil war broke out. Today, unlike the time of the Peasant Revolts, it is very difficult to crush grassroots movements because the ideals of freedom and democracy are widespread.

3. James T. Lemon, "Citizen Participation in Toronto, Late 1960s and 1970s," *Citizen Participation in Library Decisions: The Toronto Experience*, ed. John Marshall (Metuchen, NJ, & London: Scarecrow Press, 1984), 7.

4. I remember Vic Copps, the popular mayor of Hamilton, expressing these sentiments in the late 1960s, and I am told that was the position of the Old Guard Toronto politicians prior to the election of the Reform Group in 1971.

5. For a quick overview of Alinsky's twelve rules for radicals see www.bestofbeck.com/wp/activism/saul-alinskys-12-rules-for-radicals.

6. I worked as an organizer for a poor people's organization in Hamilton in late 1960 called the Hamilton Welfare Rights Organization and we used Alinsky tactics. We had a number of early successes but soon resistance emerged from politicians and welfare administrators. Toward the end of the organization we dropped confrontation as a tactic and became an advocacy group fighting for the rights of individuals who were denied social assistance.

7. I have written about this experience in an article called "Welfare Hamilton Style." Bill Freeman and Marsha Hewitt, *Their Town: The Mafia, the Media and the Party Machine* (Toronto: James Lorimer, 1979).

8. The information about Milton-Parc comes residents and from "The Destruction of Milton-Park," notes and a collection of news articles written and assembled by Dimitri Roussopoulos, www.miltonparc.org/272scans.pdf. Also from an interview with Lucia Kowalic.

9. Marion Patterson, "The Conservationists," *Montreal Calendar,* October–November 1984.

10. "Van Horne Mansion (1870–1973): A Demolition that Changed the History of Heritage Preservation," *Encyclopedia of French Cultural Heritage in North America,* www.ameriquefrancaise.org/en/article-459/Van_Horne_Mansion_(18701973):_a Demolition_That_Changed_the_History_of_Heritage_Preservation.html.

11. Ken McKenzie's M.A. thesis is the clearest analysis of the issues and events around Vancouver's freeway plan. Ken McKenzie, "Freeway Planning and Protests in Vancouver, 1954–1972," M.A. Thesis for Simon Fraser University, 1985.

12. McKenzie uses the term "ad-hoc" planning to describe the frequent changes to the Vancouver freeway plan.

13. Ibid., 80.

14. Church and Wellesley Neighbourhood Association: www.cwna.ca.

15. I have been an active participant in CommunityAIR for the last fifteen years.

CHAPTER 10: THE EXCLUDED

1. *CBC News,* "Living Conditions for First Nations 'Unacceptable': Fontaine," February 6, 2007.

2. Don Drummond and Ellen Kachuck Rosenbluth, *The Debate on First Nations Education Funding: Mind the Gap* (School of Policy Studies, Queen's University, 2013), https://qspace.library.queensu.ca/bitstream/handle/1974/14846/Drummond_et_al_2013_Debate_on_First_Nations.pdf.

3. I have done a more detailed study of poverty in my book *The New Urban Agenda: The Greater Toronto and Hamilton Area* (Toronto: Dundurn, 2015), 49–53.

4. According to press reports the Ontario government is setting up a program to test the feasibility of establishing a guaranteed annual income program, but the program will do nothing unless the rates are high enough to eliminate poverty. If that does not happen it will just be exchanging one bureaucratic welfare program with another.

5. "Canada Named as Most Tolerant Country in the World," *CTV News,* November 3, 2015.

6. "Racism Against Asian Canadians," University of Guelph, www.uoguelph.ca/diversity-human-rights/book-page/racism-against-asian-canadians.

7. Ibid.

8. "Estimate of Voter Turnout by Age Group and Gender at the 2011 Federal Election," Elections Canada, www.elections.ca/content.aspx?section=res&dir=rec/part/estim&document=index&lang=e.

9.   Education is the other major determinant as to who goes to the polls. The higher the level of education, the greater the likelihood of voting. But these figures tend to deny this. Young Canadians have much higher levels of education, on average, than those in the older age groups, but they do not vote in the same numbers.

10.   Statistics Canada, *Labour Force Survey, 1976 to 2014.*

11.   Sara Mojtehedzadeh and Laurie Monsebkraaten, "Precarious Work Is Now the New Norm, United Way Report Says," *Toronto Star*, May 21, 2015.

12.   Elaine Polfeldt, "Shocker: 40% of Workers Now Have "Contingent" Jobs, Says U.S. Government," *Forbes*, May 25, 2015.

13.   Chris Buckley, "Ontario Labour Laws Failing Vulnerable Workers," *Toronto Star*, May 1, 2016.

CHAPTER 11: DEMOCRACY, PARTICIPATION, AND SOCIAL CHANGE

1.   Dimitrios Roussopoulos and C. George Benello, *Participatory Democracy: Prospects for Democratizing Democracy* (Montreal: Black Rose Books, 2005). Murray Bookchin, *The Ecology of Freedom* (Palo Alto: Cheshire Books, 1982), http://libcom.org/files/Murray_Bookchin_The_Ecology_of_Freedom_1982.pdf.

2.   "Participation Rates in Postsecondary Education," Stats Canada, www.statcan.gc.ca/pub/81-004-x/2011004/article/11595-eng.htm#a.

3.   I have described municipal participatory democratic decision making in greater depth in my book *The New Urban Agenda*, 199–201.

4.   These are some ideas taken from Roussopoulos and Benello, *Participatory Democracy.*

5.   The most insightful insights on bureaucracy were written by Max Weber over one hundred years ago.

CHAPTER 12: CREATING A PARTICIPATORY DEMOCRACY

1.   Abraham Lincoln, "The Gettysburg Address."

APPENDIX

1.   This is a play on Saul Alinsky's *Rules for Radicals*. Alinsky was a radical. His book was an attempt to adopt radical principles and particularly explained how to use confrontation creatively to deal with community problems. I still think he was a brilliant organizer, but the issues that we are dealing with in Canada are quite different than the conditions in the poverty-stricken neighbourhoods of American cities. Canadian activists are reformist and we should give up any pretext to radical change.

INDEX